This publication was made possible by the support of the Prins Bernhard Fund

Kröller-Müller Museum

Dutch Museums (I)

Written by the staff of the museum

3rd Edition

1985

Joh. Enschedé en Zonen

Haarlem ⸱ The Netherlands

Cover:
Sailor with guitar by Chaim Jacob Lipchitz (see p.120)
Peinture/tableau by Daniel Buren
(1938, France, U.S.A.) canvas, 170 x 133 cm, 1970.

This book is a publication of
Joh. Enschedé en Zonen Grafische Inrichting B.V.,
Haarlem, The Netherlands,
accomplished with assistance from the
Kröller-Müller Foundation, Otterlo, The Netherlands.

Photography:
J. Holtman, and J. Brokerhof, Kröller-Müller Museum.

Groundplan Museum Buildings:
Architect Quist, Rotterdam.
Groundplan Museum and sculpture park:
R. M. J. M. Hoefsloot, Kröller-Müller Museum.
Total production:
Joh. Enschedé en Zonen Grafische Inrichting B.V.
Typography: Bram de Does.
English edition:
Translation by Patricia Griffiths, Amsterdam.
German edition:
Translation by Gabriele Kreusch, Brussel.
French edition:
Translation by Claude Girard, Amsterdam.

ISBN: 90 70024 04 7

Preface

The book about the Kröller-Müller Museum that Ellen Joosten, Deputy Director, wrote in 1965* went out of print long ago and since then there has existed a need for a similar publication, in which the history of the museum and its collections would be told anew, partly in the light of what has happened in the intervening period. Thus we gladly acceded to Enschedé's proposal that a book should be produced about the museum which would be more than a brief guide, while still remaining within the reach of people with a genuine interest. We were all the more pleased to do this since it was possible for publication to coincide with the opening of the extension to the museum.

The texts are by members of staff, Auke van der Woud, Curator, describing the history of the museum and the collection, Ellen Joosten dealing with the sculptures and sculptors' drawings and Paul Hefting, Curator, with the paintings and the drawings associated with them. Virtually all the photographs reproduced in the book have been taken by J. Holtman, Head of the Technical Services Department. The book is published in Dutch, English and German editions simultaneously.

It gives us very great pleasure that the unity of the Kröller-Müller Museum and the Hoge Veluwe National Park should once again find expression in this book, the essence of that unity being the harmony between nature, architecture and art that the founders wanted to create.

Rudolf W. Oxenaar
Director, Kröller-Müller Museum

* The Kröller-Müller Museum (Museums discovered, series edited by Sir John Rothenstein), Shorewood Publishers, Inc., New York, 1965.

Preface to the second edition

This book was originally published just too early to be fully up to date as regards the museum's extensive new wing and the latest additions to the permanent collection of sculpture.

The need for a second edition within three years, in itself an indication of the book's popularity, has given us the opportunity to be more explicit about the new building and to make considerable additions to the description of the collections. The new texts required have been written by a temporary member of our staff, Fred Wagemans. The number of reproductions remains the same, but the emphasis now falls more on the newer and newest acquisitions, especially in the field of sculpture.

R. O. 1980

Contents

Groundplan museum   8
Groundplan sculpture park with surroundings   10

THE HISTORY
The building   11
The collection   30

ILLUSTRATIONS
Paintings   41
Drawings   102
Sculptures   116
Sculpture park   138

Groundplan museum

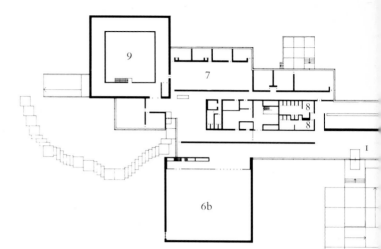

Key

1 Entrance
2 Entrances to sculpture park
3 Exhibition areas
4 Restaurant
5 Sales area for reproductions
6a Small auditorium
6b Dr.C.H. van der Leeuw auditorium
7 Library
8 Toilets
9 Store

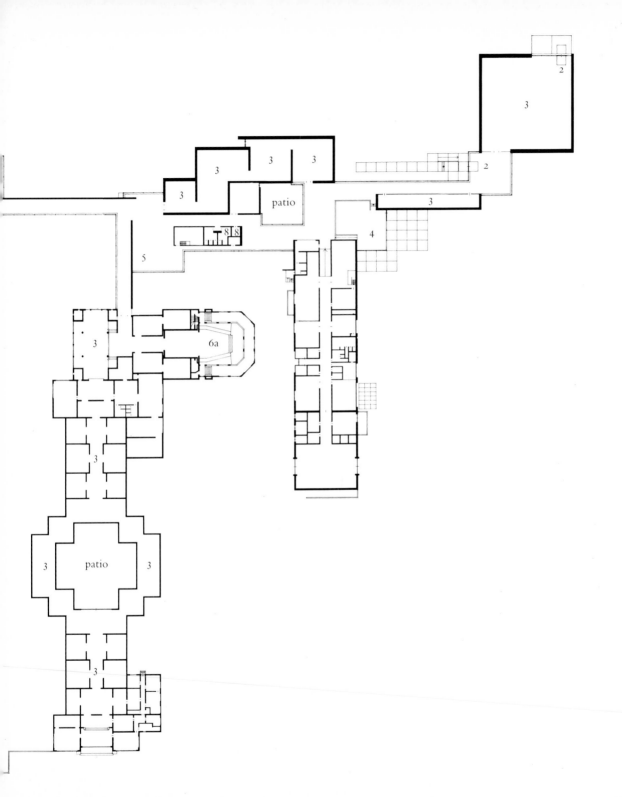

2

3

3

3

3

2

patio

3

8 8

5

4

3

6a

3

3

patio

3

3

3

9

Groundplan sculpture park with surroundings

0 10 20 30 40 50 m

The history

The building

'On the strength of its inventory the 'Galerie Kröller' is the greatest of all modern Dutch private collections. The catalogue lists 669 paintings and drawings. In spiritual respects, too, it is in the leading position in a certain sense, for the mere fact of its existence has given other amateurs of art the courage to set themselves to acquire the work of contemporaries', so wrote F. M. Hübner in his *Moderne Kunst in den Holländischen Privatsammlungen* (1921). The collection could be seen at 1 Lange Voorhout in The Hague on Mondays and Fridays between 10 a.m. and 4 p.m., but only on production of an admission ticket 'obtainable on written application from the collector herself'. The collector was, of course, Mrs. Hélène Kröller-Müller.

Of German origin, she was born in Horst near Essen in 1869. Her father, Wilhelm Heinrich Müller, had a small iron-smeltery there at the time, but shortly afterwards he set up a shipping and trading firm in Düsseldorf with a branch office in Rotterdam. The Rotterdam office was headed by Willem Kröller, a son of a contractor who was a partner of Müller's. Willem sent his younger brother Anton to the office in Düsseldorf to learn the business. There he got to know Hélène Müller and in 1888 they married, just after he had become head of the Rotterdam branch of the firm following the death of his brother. When his father-in-law also died in 1889, Anton Kröller found himself at the age of twenty-seven at the head of the firm of Wm. H. Müller & Co. He was evidently a brilliant businessman, for within a decade or two he had built up his firm into a powerful international concern with large-scale interests in shipping, the corn trade in America and the exploitation of mineral mines, mainly in Spain and North Africa. The fortunes he made lent wings to his wife's ideal: the formation of a great art collection which would be devoted in particular to contemporary art. By 1921 this collection was the largest of all the private collections of modern art in the Netherlands, but it was to become still larger. In 1933 it comprised over 4,000 drawings, around 275 sculptures and many hundreds of paintings, mostly of high quality.

That Hélène Kröller began collecting was principally due to the lessons in art appreciation she had received from H.P. Bremmer. Bremmer taught people how to understand art, giving courses in fifteen or so places throughout the country from Groningen to Eindhoven. 'The aim of this course is to give an introduction to the works of the Fine Arts from earliest times up to the present day and to do so more by means of critical comparison than by following the method of modern textbooks of art history. The teaching will be given mainly by means of illustrative examples and everyone will be quite free to put up his own opinion against mine, in order by so doing to arrive at a better understanding of artistic values.' Bremmer also gave a course of this type at his own home in The Hague and in 1907 Mrs. Kröller enrolled for it. It was a revelation to her. 'He gave me my first insight into art. He showed me the way to distinguish the wheat from the chaff in art.' Throughout her life he was to remain 'my adviser on all aesthetic questions.'

As a result of Bremmer's lessons she very soon felt the need to collect for herself examples of the art that came up for discussion in his teaching. Nor was that all. Now that she was better able to appreciate what she found beautiful, she also became more aware of what she found ugly: the house she lived in (*Huize Ten Vijver* in Scheveningen) began to be a source of mortification to her, for its design now seemed to her to be dull and commonplace. She began to long for a house that would be specially designed for her by a good architect. After a stay of some weeks in Florence in 1910, where she saw that the powerful Medici were still living on centuries later in their buildings and in the works of art bought or created to their commission, her mind was made up. She went to Berlin to meet Professor Peter Behrens, whose work she had got to know from periodicals on modern architecture, since he had aroused a great deal of interest by reason of his striking work for AEG. In the spring of 1911 he came to Scheveningen and accepted the commission to design a country house for Mr. and Mrs. Kröller-Müller. It was to be built on the *Ellenwoude* estate at Wassenaar. Behrens made plans for a house in lucid, cubical architecture, rather simple in design, but certainly representative (fig. 1). When his design had been finalized, Hélène Kröller had a feeling that he had not, after all, understood what she wanted. To set her mind at rest her husband had the design carried out as a mock-up – a full-scale construction of wood and painted canvas on rails which could be moved about on the proposed site. That clinched matters: this design, which already included a gallery for the collection that had grown appreciably in the meanwhile, was not to be realized.

1. Design for the country house *Ellenwoude*, Wassenaar (1911).
Architect: Peter Behrens (1868–1940).

The commission now went to the young Ludwig Mies van der Rohe, who had set up as an independent architect after breaking with Behrens, his previous employer, while the *Ellenwoude* project was in progres. To be on the safe side and at Bremmer's instigation, H. P. Berlage was also asked to draw up plans, Bremmer regarding him as a great architect. By September 1912 both men had finished their drawings and maquettes. Superficially Mies' plan looked very much like that of Behrens – his architecture, too, was determined by long rectangular planes devoid of ornament (fig. 2). But this new country house had none of the stiff importance of Behrens' design, the outside walls were lower and the building spread itself out in space, whereas in Behrens' plan the rooms together formed a compact, closed ground plan. Berlage designed a country house that, to tell the truth, looked more like a seminary (fig. 3). It had a main building with two wings at rightangles to it. The sombre whole made a somewhat complicated impression with its numerous different roof forms (there was even a little bell tower), outbuildings and arcades. When the time came to make the choice between Berlage and Mies, Bremmer played the leading role. S. van Deventer gave an eye-witness account of the occasion: 'Bremmer looked long and attentively first at the sketches, then at the maquettes. At last he pointed to Berlage's work and said, "That is art," and at Mies' work, "That is not". And then, with intense feeling, his arguments poured forth like a tidal wave. He gave vent to an impassioned plea for Berlage and a destructive criticism of the design by Mies'. Mrs. Kröller was anything but pleased with Bremmer's judgement, but after the design by Mies had also been built in wood and canvas, she declared that he was right. However, she did so only reluctantly and probably not entirely wholeheartedly, for Berlage's *Ellenwoude* was not built either.

Berlage had won international renown for his Stock Exchange building in Amsterdam (1898–1903) and he was recognized as the leading light of modern architecture in the Netherlands, but that had not yet brought him a thriving practice. When the municipality of Rotterdam disappointed him – and actually his supporters as well – by not inviting him to enter the competition for the new town hall on the Coolsingel, Kröller took him, in 1913, into the service of both the firm and himself and his wife personally, with a contract that was intended to last for at least ten years. It now seems somewhat bewildering that Berlage, who made no secret of his socialist sympathies either in speaking or writing, should have placed himself at the command of such a copybook capitalist entrepreneur, but it must be remembered that his socialism was of a different complexion from that of today and also that Mrs. Kröller was receptive to ideals directed at bringing art to society in general, ideals which Berlage most certainly subscribed to. In addition there was for Berlage the highly practical consideration that the contract offered him a secure living and the chance of interesting, large-scale commissions. For

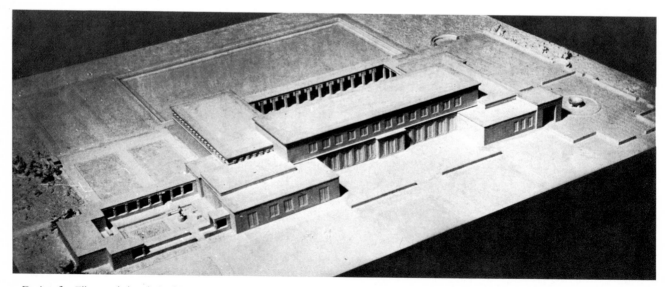

2. Design for *Ellenwoude* (1912). Architect: Ludwig Mies van der Rohe (1886–1969).

3. Design for *Ellenwoude* (1913). Architect: H.P. Berlage (1856–1934).

Kröller himself the affair also had a personal angle, for 'chuckling to himself (he said): "What will Rotterdam make of it? They have treated him badly, but now we shall just see to it that he comes into his own again"'.

Berlage was given an office in the building at 1 Lange Voorhout, of which the ground floor was installed as Hélène Kröller's museum. His collaboration with her was not without its problems, especially on the personal level, and after some years of it he was longing to be independent again. In 1919 the contract was prematurely ended, Berlage having in the six intervening years designed furniture, lamps, schemes of decoration, tableware, cutlery and buildings. Immediately after entering Kröller's service he had made plans for a new office building for the Müller firm in London, 'Holland House', which had a daring modern façade and office space that could be divided up as required by movable walls. At the same time he built a large farmhouse, *De Schipborg*, near Zuidlaren, where the Kröllers' eldest son set up as a gentleman-farmer. It was intended to be a model farm and from letters to Berlage from Mrs. Kröller it appears that he was required to gain an idea of how to give form to this ambitious project from foreign publications. But the best commission came after that – a hunting-box mainly for the convenience of Mr. Kröller, and a museum with living-quarters for his wife, to be sited not far from each other on the Hoge Veluwe.

With the purchase of the Hoge Veluwe, a wide expanse of heathy and wooded country in the Province of Gelderland, the Kröllers had become large landowners. It had all begun in a fairly modest way with Hélène Kröller's buying *De Harskamp* on the Veluwe, a somewhat tumbledown farmhouse with 450 hectares of land. Two reasons come to mind for this

4. The *St. Hubertus* hunting-box, Hoenderloo (1914–20). Architect: H.P. Berlage.

purchase, which seems a rather surprising one for an art-loving Hague lady – she was mad on horse-riding in the Veluwe landscape and she was truly feudal in her attitudes. She sometimes took better care, so tradition would have us believe, of her horses and dogs than her servants and having the direction of a small army of peasant-farmers and foresters must have afforded her deep satisfaction. And so, all idyllically, she set up a little house there, *Het Klaverblad,* with 'a single living room with an open fire over which hung a copper kettle. There was a little kitchen with a range, just like you find in the farmhouses all over the Veluwe'. That was in 1909. Within the next seven years Mr. Kröller had bought the whole area of the present Hoge Veluwe National Park, comprising around 6800 hectares, primarily in order to be able to indulge in horse-riding and hunting there, but also in order to keep this still almost untouched area of natural landscape out of the hands of industrialists, who undoubtedly saw it as a possible place to set up in since the price of land there was extremely low. Mr. Kröller had a public road diverted and fenced off his land so that the deer, the wild boar and the specially introduced moufflon would remain available for hunting purposes. Now that the centre of gravitiy of the Kröller possessions had shifted to the Veluwe, the ambitious building plans were diverted there too.

A start was made with the hunting-box (fig. 4). Berlage must surely have had things to his liking at that stage, for the demands made on him were high and the means virtually unlimited. True, the First World War was raging outside the Netherlands, but that was all grist to the mill of Müller & Co. with their specialist corn and mining interests. 'Business was exceptionally good. Those were the years of the war profits', wrote the Kröllers' biographer, S. van Deventer, almost too candidly. The hunting-box was named *St. Hubertus* after the patron saint of the chase. It became a complex including a dining-room, a library, a billiard-room, bedrooms and accommodation for guests. The interior was appointed expensively, but without excess, Berlage drawing the designs for the new tableware, cutlery and a great deal of furniture. Naturally this was always done in close consultation with Hélène Kröller and it was probably also she who wanted the architecture to symbolize the legend of St. Hubert. St. Hubert, so the legend relates, was converted from an all too passionate huntsman into a believer during a hunting-party, when a stag appeared before him with a shining golden cross between its antlers, as a warning that he ought to make a serious improvement in his way of life. The ground plan of the hunting-box represented the antlers, the tall tower the cross. 'The hall has been kept dark and sombre, a mood of melancholy prevailing there. This is the symbol of the first, dark period of St. Hubert's life, which was made sombre by the wickedness and ferocity that governed him then. The passage under the tower (is) the way from darkness to light, for, after all, it was through his encounter with the cross that St. Hubert's life made the transition from turbulence to tranquillity, that he passed out of darkness into the fullness of light.' The library was a symbolic interpretation 'of the period spent by St. Hubert in the cloister. The tall windows bring out a feeling of seclusion and solitude here'. But in the tea-room 'a completely different atmosphere predominates. The seclusion revealed by the library is now over. In accordance with the legend St. Hubert's monastic days have now passed by. Light shines in freely from all sides and it is one of the brightest and sunniest rooms in the house'. The symbolic climax came – not entirely unexpectedly in view of Mrs. Kröller's personality – in that lady's sitting-room, 'which represents the peak of wisdom and tranquillity achieved, the symbol of the clear conscience'.

The hunting-box was finished in 1920, it having been longer in building than anticipated owing to the scarcity of materials during the war. But the museum-cum-house still existed only on paper. Mrs. Kröller had decided that her collection was to be put on display on the Veluwe, where the confrontation between nature and culture was stark and inescapable, and the old plan of presenting it in Wassenaar had gone by the board. In 1916 Berlage was commissioned to design plans for a

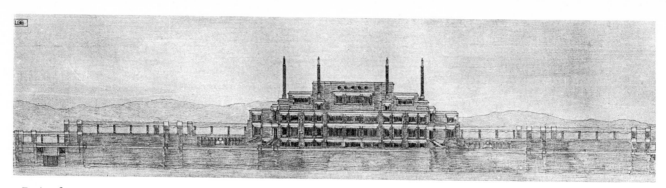

5. Design for a museum on the Hoge Veluwe, near the Franse Berg; south elevation (1917). Architect: H. P. Berlage.

building at the foot of the Franse Berg, from where at that time one could still look out over endless expanses of sand (which are now much more overgrown). He designed a large building with a gallery for the Van Goghs in the centre surrounded by small rooms for the other paintings, an enclosed sculpture garden and a hall for lectures and plays. The living-quarters were sited high up in order to get the view over the game preserve and the whole complex was largely surrounded by terraces and gardens (fig. 5). But before these plans could be brought to a definitive stage, Berlage broke off his contract with the Kröllers. He is said to have done so in order to regain his freedom, but the fact that he gave up such a visionary project as the museum building would surely seem to indicate that he must have been at his wits' end, whatever the reason for it may have been.

Shortly afterwards, in September 1919, Mrs. Kröller had some contact with the architect A. J. Kropholler, who gladly took on the contract for the Five Houses at Hoenderloo – five dwellings for staff – but fought shy of that for the museum. In October she concluded an agreement with Henry van de Velde (1863–1957), whose work she had already admired earlier on a visit to the collector Osthaus in Hagen (Westphalia), and whom, now that his work had become 'quieter', she regarded as eminently suited to give form to her plans. Four days after concluding this agreement she was already writing, 'Van de Velde builds music, Berlage forces walls to rise for you', a somewhat heartless pronounce-ment in view of St. Hubertus, but it certainly indicates that she was greatly taken with her new collaborator. And Van de Velde was equally taken with her and her husband. The first time he was with them on the Veluwe he was, so he wrote later, 'almost in a state of intoxication and ready to sign my name to anything that those two people, who had brought me to this paradise, wanted of me'. He moved from Switzerland to Wassenaar, built himself a house there and remained in the service of the Kröllers until 1926.

Van de Velde was given an office in the place vacated by Berlage shortly before, on the third floor of 1 Lange Voorhout. No sooner had the first drawings for the museum been made than Mrs. Kröller was already saying enthusiastically that Berlage's design paled into insignificance by comparison. The presentation drawings show a museum in a severe, closed form, almost a fortress with its strong walls and windows like holes (fig. 6) and completely different from Berlage's plan in which the outside walls were designed precisely to be entirely open. The two designs reveal two opposite conceptions of the museum. Berlage felt that people inside the museum must be able to see outside and vice versa; Van de Velde isolated the art collection so that people could concentrate on looking at it in complete peace.

In building the museum money was no object, at least so it seemed at that moment. 'The estimate is in; I read the figure of six million without the terraces. I read it and quickly clapped the two pages together.' Building began; after one year, in 1922, part of the concrete substructure had been completed and 4,000 cubic metres of Maulbronner sandstone for the cladding of the outside had been brought in on specially laid railway lines – and there the whole business came to a stop. The international economic recession brought great losses in its train for Müller & Co. and that spelt the end of this project. The complete specifications for the building – *i.e.* a large number of drawings, a good thousand at a careful estimate – and a rather lost concrete wall at the foot of the Franse Berg are all that remain of it now.

6. Design for a museum on the Hoge Veluwe, near the Franse Berg (1920). Architect: Henry van de Velde (1863–1957).

Van de Velde continued to work for the Kröllers for another four years. He built the farmhouse and outbuildings, *De Harskamp,* for the eldest son and designed the furniture for it and for the firm he built an office and sheds in Rotterdam and directed the rebuilding and installation of several other offices. He designed publicity material, book covers, furniture and table-silver and as late as 1930 he built a villa in Wassenaar, *Groot Haesebroek,* for the couple who had taken no further pains over a new house since the failure of the commission given to Behrens and Mies van der Rohe.

It is a remarkable fact that even though the extensive and expensive plans she had envisaged for the museum had been shipwrecked, Hélène Kröller did not give up her ideal. Only it was now definitely established that the matter would have to be approached in a different way. The economic crisis had made it clear that the personal property of the Kröllers, and that including *St. Hubertus,* the art collection and the estate on the Veluwe, was extremely vulnerable and that if Müller & Co., which Kröller had always refused to turn into a limited liability company, were to be hit again by a more serious crisis, there was a danger that that property would be sold and split up. In order to prevent that, the Kröller-Müller Foundation was set up in 1928. It was intended, 'for the use and enjoyment of the community', to administer the Hoge Veluwe estate, the buildings on it and Hélène Kröller's collection and to strive for the foundation of a museum where that collection could be arranged and shown to the public. With this foundation, which was largely governed by the Kröller family, the private possessions became in principle public property. In 1935 a further step was taken with the setting up of a new foundation, the Hoge Veluwe National Park, which bought the Hoge Veluwe estate for f 800,000, the State making a high mortgage available on favourable terms. At the same time the art collection was given to the State, but only on condition that the State would within five years build a museum for it, which it was stipulated must be designed by Henry van de Velde. In addition it was laid down that the collection, either as a whole or in part, might not be shown outside the Hoge Veluwe, except in the form of temporary loans for exhibitions.

From as early as 1911 Mrs. Kröller had wanted a separate museum for the collection she was engaged in building up and she never thereafter thought of selling it either as a whole or in part or of housing it in an existing museum. Like so many of the powerful people of the past, she had linked architects, artists and works of art with her name. The treasures of the Medici had shown her in 1910 what that could lead to: to immortality in a certain sense. Whether she also wanted to gain immortality in that way is not known for certain, but it certainly sometimes seems as if she did. 'I am not collecting for present possession', she wrote in 1912, 'but I always think of the future in connection with what I collect, in the sense of how far the work will be able to stand the test of the future.' When she was no longer able to collect very much, she applied all her energies to keeping her collection and the estate on the Veluwe together and making them inviolable. She achieved her aim by putting her possessions, under certain conditions, into the hands of the community, the only kind of owner that, to the individual, seems timeless.

In the poverty-stricken thirties it was impossible even to hope that Van de Velde's large-scale design could be carried out. He was therefore commissioned by the State to design a much smaller and cheaper museum, and this was built in 1937–38 as a job creation project for unemployed building workers from Arnhem. It was sited not at the foot of the Franse Berg, but a short distance away in the wood, for it was meant to be a temporary home which would be superseded when better times came to make it possible to build the large museum on the original site. That times never would become better in that respect was a positive certainty after the Second World War and so the building that was regarded as a temporary museum is the Kröller-Müller Museum of today (fig. 7, 8). It was directed by Hélène Kröller until her death in December 1939.

7. Kröller-Müller Museum, Otterlo (1937–38, with extension of 1953).
Architect: Henry van de Velde. Photograph: Aero-Camera, Rotterdam.

8. Kröller-Müller Museum, interior.

Van de Velde gave the museum a simple and convenient ground plan, which is in fact based on the old plan for the large museum. It was centred – like all the previous plans – on the Van Gogh collection, which is shown here round a courtyard. From the entrance to the museum (which is now no longer in use) one came first to six small rooms with works of art created before Van Gogh's time, and after the Van Gogh rooms there were a further six small rooms for works of the period after 1870. In the exhibition area there were very few windows. This ensured that the wall surfaces were as large as possible and it is also because of this that the experience of nature as opposed to culture became so powerful. Van de Velde concentrated that experience at three points, at the entrance, which he designed as a glass wall, at the courtyard, which he wanted to make visible from the interior of the museum by glass walls on three sides, but where Mrs. Kröller considered that one wall was enough, and at what was then the back of the building. There shortly after 1938 he designed a sculpture gallery with two walls that are virtually entirely of glass. The building of this was held up by the war, but it was finished in 1953, as was the wing on the sculpture gallery with an auditorium and extra exhibition space, Van de Velde's last work.

Later an attempt was also made in a different way to find possibilities of bringing art and nature together. In 1961 the first part of the sculpture garden behind the museum, designed by Professor J. T. P. Bijhouwer, was opened. The exhibiting of sculptures in the open air was an idea that had aroused great interest after the Second World War. Exhibitions had been held in Battersea Park in London since 1949 and in Sonsbeek Park in Arnhem since 1951, while Antwerp had had a permanent collection as well as exhibitions of sculpture in Middelheim Park since 1950. For that matter, Mrs. Kröller had also started to do this, albeit on a much smaller scale, as early as 1915. She had commissioned Mendes da Costa to make a monument in the north of the Hoge Veluwe to Christiaan de Wet, General in the Boer War, and she had had Henry van de Velde lay out a garden complex with a monumental bench opposite the present museum in honour of Martinus Steijn, who was President of the Orange Free State from 1896 to 1902 and for whom, like De Wet, she had a great respect. In addition she had had Chinese and Japanese sculpture set up in the 'museum avenue' not far from the present café, *De Koperen Kop*. The sculpture park, which was thus a continuation of her initiative, now occupies eleven hectares and accommodates about sixty sculptures.

Around 1965 the fact that the museum had been built as a temporary structure had become all too clear. In practical and aesthetic respects it was eminently satisfactory, the lighting problem in particular having been solved in an exemplary way by a simple roof construction, but the heating system, which had been built into the ceilings in a highly inventive and unobtrusive manner, was almost worn out and the 'climate' inside the building could no longer be kept under adequate control. Sometimes it was too dry there and often much too humid. In addition the foundations of the museum had only been designed for temporary use and they were thus incapable of standing up to a lengthy existence, with the result that the struggle against the constantly recurring cracks in the wall had become a battle against hopeless odds. Between 1970 and 1972 the building was subjected to a thorough restoration and equipped with air-conditioning. Since then it has been not a temporary, but the definitive home of the art collection and it has even been listed as a historical monument.

This establishment of the definitive character of the museum building immediately involved the recognition that the space problem, which had already been growing for years, must be solved by building a sizable extension. However, while there was admittedly room enough round

Ill. 9–15: the extension of 1972. Architect: W. G. Quist. Photos by Jan and Fridtjof Versnel.

the Van de Velde building, not every site was suitable, since it was felt that that building must remain intact and clearly visible as an independent entity. The solution came with the idea that the existing collection could be 'turned round' from the chronological point of view. Since the time of Mrs. Kröller's directorship visitors had seen the earlier art first, following in it the development towards the art of their own time. Now they encounter the contemporary art first and proceed backwards from there through its previous history. This completely different confrontation has been achieved not by rehanging the collection, but by changing the position of the entrance (fig. p. 8,9). The path that leads to it runs parallel to the old building, thus allowing the rhythm of that building's architectural volumes to be experienced as a whole with great clarity. The architect of the new extension, W. G. Quist, has respected Van de Velde's architecture in other ways too, perhaps most of all by giving his own architecture a character entirely of its own, which is thus quite different from that of Van de Velde's.

10.

The extension (1972, 1975–77), which is placed at right-angles to the long axis of the old building, is rounded off at both ends with a relatively large architectural feature, the new auditorium on the one side and the large sculpture gallery on the other. The harmony in the contours of the new building is thus of quite a different nature – a dynamic alternation of high and low, of widening out and narrowing – from that which Mrs. Kröller asked of Van de Velde in the past, which was, after all, based on symmetry in both his museum plans. The old and new buildings differ externally in their colour as well, the walls of the former being of light brown brick, those of the latter of concrete brick that is almost white. The colour contrast is not, however, an especially hard one. Quist has fitted the new building into the existing vegetation (and, indeed, also adapted it to the differences in height of the terrain) with great care and discretion, so that it is largely hidden behind the trees. With the extension, and especially with the right wing, the museum building now stretches out towards the sculpture park, with the result that a strong link has been forged between the collection inside and that outside. How close the connection between nature and architecture is in the new building is revealed in the interior, where the walls are either entirely of brick or entirely of glass from floor to ceiling. There are a large number of these glass walls and this too is a contrast with the old building, the interior of which, apart from Van de Velde's sculpture gallery, nowhere affords a view of the external surroundings. In this connection it must be remembered that what Van de Velde built was virtually confined to a series of linked exhibition areas (primarily for paintings), with hardly any service accommodation, since this was scarely needed in that 'temporary' museum with its small staff. The new extension, on the other hand, has many more functions: there are offices, work places, stores, a library, a large auditorium and a sales area for reproductions and catalogues, as well as the exhibition areas that also find a place in it. In short, then, the old and new parts of the building are quite different not only in character, but in part in purpose too. They also house different collections. In the old building is shown the original Kröller-Müller collection, while the new accommodates sculptures, reliefs and drawings of after 1950 or thereabouts.

Van de Velde's symmetrical building with its numerous small exhibition rooms is a follow-up to the traditional museum architecture of the 19th century, while Quist has in principle built on the legacy of *De Stijl* and the *Nieuwe Zakelijkheid*. Nevertheless, the old and new parts of the museum do have some essential things in common. Both show a careful handling of detail and both have a simplicity that has been finely calculated to the last degree. And it is precisely through this simplicity that they have both become architecture that fascinates by reason of relationships, relationships between planes, dimensions, light and shadow and materials.

11. Photo: M.E. Jurrissen.

12.

13.

14.

15.

The collection

Right from the start Mrs. Kröller was deeply impressed by Bremmer's lessons in art appreciation and one of the results of this was that she also wanted to have for herself the paintings and sculptures he discussed in them. She made her first important purchase in 1909: three paintings by Vincent van Gogh, *Sunflowers, The sower* and a still life, *Bottle with lemons*. In the years that followed she was to amass a tremendous collection of paintings and drawings by him. Like her husband she had acquired a taste for hunting, only in her case it was hunting for works of art. In April 1912, for instance, she was in Paris with Bremmer. At an art-dealers he found five paintings good enough to buy: 'He bought them with an offer – a third of the asking price – and went out trembling like a leaf, so pleased was he with his haul'. That was before lunch. After it Bremmer again went out and bought for his patroness another painting and two more drawings by Van Gogh and a painting by Seurat. Later that afternoon, strolling in the Latin Quarter, they found a medieval wooden head of Christ in a little shop full of old bits and pieces... The next day Mrs. Kröller went to visit Signac in his studio and she bought a painting by him and one by his friend Seurat. A month later she bought two Corots, two Daumiers and two important Van Goghs at a sale.

She mostly bought from Dutch art-dealers (d'Audretsch, C. M. van Gogh, Komter, Huinck), but she also went to Cassirer and Flechtheim in Germany, Giroux in Brussels and Druet and Léonce Rosenberg in Paris. She bought a great deal at sales too and sometimes from the artists themselves, in both cases via Bremmer in the main. Although she was able to buy many outstanding works of art at a moment when the prices they were fetching were still relatively low, her collecting activities naturally cost an enormous amount of money. 'Now we go from the credit to the debit side', Mr. Kröller is said to have muttered good-naturedly on many occasions as he went from his offices to his wife's rooms in the premises at 1–3 Lange Voorhout. The economic crisis of 1922, which sent the firm's returns plummeting, spelt the end of large-scale collecting. Thus Mrs. Kröller acquired far and away the largest part of her collection in the short period between 1908 and 1922. It was one of the first important collections of modern art in the world.

She had built it up with a definite aim in mind: 'in making a choice each canvas has to stand the test of fitting into the context of the whole'. Thus she did not buy 'at random'. The whole was intended to give a picture of those developments in painting that she regarded as being of importance for the future and in this connection we would do well to remember that to collect mainly contemporary art – which was sometimes so new that public opinion about it was either negative or non-existent – with this aim in view demanded daring and vision. What Mrs. Kröller's vision was clearly emerges from her *Beschouwingen over problemen in de ontwikkeling der moderne schilderkunst* (Observations on problems in the development of modern painting), which she wrote on the basis of her collection and published in book-form in 1925. She was not particularly interested in art-historical facts and she did not consider it important to set out the details of all the stylistic periods there were or had been and how they had arisen. Her aim was rather to make it clear that there are two conceptions in art: 'They form a contrast that is very ancient and that in fact always existed: there is a realistic and an idealistic movement in the sphere of art'. Realists and idealists both started from observable reality. Realists were primarily concerned with observation: the play of light, effects of colour, shade and perspective, the rendering of textures. Idealists were not so much taken up with the concrete manifestation of reality, but they 'recast' it according to their personal temperaments and feelings. They heightened or toned down colours and sometimes abstracted the forms, thus giving a picture of their 'idea' of reality.

As Hélène Kröller-Müller saw it realism and idealism had always alternated with one another in art, in accordance with the prevailing 'spirit of the age'. In the development of modern art, which began in the late 19th century, these two movements had come to the fore more clearly than ever as contrasts – for example, in Impressionism as opposed to Cubism. But in spite of this Mrs. Kröller could not regard the development of modern art as a movement towards two extremes. She believed that in the future there would be a synthesis between realism and idealism, and this she termed the 'realism of the synthesis'. It was on this idea that her collecting was based. More than that, it was an integral part of her whole philosophy of life. She was actually writing about herself when she wrote in her book about a painter 'who stands before things with a childlike awe,... in the deeper insight that the solution to the enigma of life can never be found in a one-sided way: neither in Spirituality nor Materialism, since one would thus have to posit a duality of spirit and matter, which is incompatible with the essence of the Absolute and unthinkable', for she herself was firmly convinced that there could be no future for man's spiritual development unless he realised that spirit and matter are one. Spirituality and materialism as ways of thinking and idealism and realism as currents in art were each, on their own and as one-sided approaches, dead ends in her view.

She owed this idea in part, perhaps, to philosophical insights that were fairly new at that time, such as those of the physiologist Max Verworn, for example, who had gone into the link between spirit and matter in his *Naturwissenschaft und Weltanschauung* (1904): 'I take a stone in my hand. What do I know about it? It is heavy – that is an observation –, it is cold – also an observation –, it is hard – again an observation –, it has a form – a complex of observations –, it falls and moves – likewise a complex of observations. Thus in reality the antithesis between the material world and the spirit simply does not exist at all, since the material world is only the content of the spirit'. Mrs. Kröller mentioned Verworn as 'one of the writers for whom I really had some use and who have made me', and we can now certainly see why. Verworn had already demonstrated by reasoned argument that spirit and matter are one, a statement which, translated into Latin as *Spiritus et Materia Unum,* was later to become Mrs. Kröller's motto.

This was the realm of ideas in which the Kröller-Müller collection was originally formed: works of art by 'realists' and 'idealists' and the precursors of the spirit of the age of the near future, the 'realists of the synthesis'. That meant, to come down to brass tacks and name a few names, the purchase of work by, for example, Millet, Weissenbruch, Gabriel, Israels, Breitner, Renoir and Fantin Latour, whom Mrs. Kröller regarded as realists; of paintings by Redon, Signac, Seurat and Toorop, to represent the transition from realism to idealism; and of the work of Picasso, Gris, Herbin, Mondriaan and Van der Leck as representatives of idealism. Herbin and perhaps also Van der Leck were designated by her as representing the 'realism of the synthesis', albeit with some hesitation as she was still not entirely sure of herself. There were also a few artists whom she did not include in these groups, but placed above them, principally Vincent van Gogh, whose work formed the core of her collection. He was, after all, pre-eminently one of the 'great spirits of our modern art, on whom the spirit of the age had no hold, because their own personalities revealed themselves so powerfully in them'.

16. Cornelis Veth (1880–1962), 'Bremmer must have his say'. (Kröller-Müller Museum Collection.)

It cannot be accepted of Mrs. Kröller, whose life and thoughts were so intensely bound up with art, that she would have allowed her collection to be built up by others, *i.e.* by Bremmer. This has certainly been suggested. 'Bremmer must have his say', scoffed Cornelis Veth with a drawing (fig. 16) on which a lackey is holding a painting that is being looked at by Mrs. Kröller (sitting peering through a lorgnette) and Bremmer (standing with his hands in his pockets), whom one can almost hear saying once again, 'That is art. That is not.' Although Henry van de Velde widened Mrs. Kröller's field of vision, there are many things that make it clear that Bremmer made a mark on the collection. And, indeed, there are other private collections created in the Netherlands at that time which reveal Bremmer's influence in their composition. He had a great reputation at that period, when people were undoubtedly willing to buy modern art, if only they could see a reason for doing so, and he provided various collectors with a reason through his inspiring interpretations. He described himself as an art educationalist and he not only gave a great many lectures and courses, but from 1903 on, in order to reach a still wider audience, he also published a periodical with large reproductions and accompanying texts, entitled *Moderne Kunstwerken.* That publication was given up in 1910, but in 1913 he started another periodical, *Beeldende Kunst,* in which, up to the last volume in 1932, he now discussed not only modern art, but earlier art as well. The choice of works of art dealt with there shows a striking similarity to the nature of the Kröller-Müller collection at the same period. In that collection the 'Bremmerians', friends and pupils of Bremmer (who himself painted for a while), are relatively strongly represented: Zandleven, Van Hettinga Tromp, Verster, Mendes da Costa, Raedecker, and Bart van der Leck.

Van der Leck is a case apart. Bremmer paid him a visit in 1912, afterwards buying various paintings from him, a number of which he resold to Mrs. Kröller. As a result of this contact Van der Leck was taken into the service of the firm of Müller & Co. in 1914, primarily to concern himself with designing colour schemes for the buildings belonging to the firm. This he did until 1916. In the two years after that he concluded a contract with Mrs. Kröller, whereby she acquired the option of purchasing the work he produced and after that he again got a contract of the same sort from Bremmer, this time for a longer period, up to 1945. During that period, too, Mrs. Kröller bought work by him via Bremmer, with the result that the Kröller-Müller Museum now has an imposing Van der Leck collection: 42 paintings and around 400 drawings.

Mrs. Kröller had a great admiration for Van der Leck's art, primarily because, in her view, he succeeded to such perfection in abstracting his subjects to such an extent that the representations of them no longer had any individual characteristics, but had become timeless and placeless, pure 'idea'. Mondriaan had a similar method of work for a while and Mrs. Kröller bought paintings by him as well, again via Bremmer, who had a contract with him from 1914 to 1918. But when Mondriaan's work became completely abstract and the last trace of observable reality disappeared from his paintings, Mrs. Kröller's interest in him also disappeared. 'Art is battle over the object', so she thought, and Mondriaan had lost that battle. She now founds his work too 'emotional', by which she evidently meant too one-sidedly in the realm of the spirit, since it no longer had any connection with matter.

This was probably also the reason for her lack of any deep interest in the work of the *De Stijl* movement, which was scarcely represented in her collection. The Expressionists, too, were refused admission to it: they were also no longer engaged in doing battle over the object, since they were clearly concerned only with the expression of their feelings.

With the Cubists, however, things were quite different. Mrs. Kröller liked their work for the same reasons as she admired that of Van der Leck. She bought her first Cubist painting in Paris in 1913, a still life by Gris. It was also the first Cubist work that she had ever seen and as a description written by her reveals, although she was surprised by it, she understood the painter's intention immediately. When, during a course of lectures on modern art she gave in The Hague in 1924, she wanted to make the principles of Cubism clear to her audience, she well understood what problems she would be creating. 'Seeing modern things always has a very painful side, because they throw us off balance inwardly, almost subvert us and compel us to look at the old afresh, to fathom the new and to estimate both at their true value. In all probability one will have as a result to bid farewell to much that one previously thought beautiful.' This had, after all, been her own experience, as, for instance, on one occasion in Paris, in 1922: 'We also went to visit Léger, one of the leading Cubists. Nothing else in Paris made such an impression on me as his work, although I must in honesty confess that for the first five minutes I stood before it in dismay'.

It almost goes without saying that she bought work not only by the great masters, but also by less important artists. She did this partly to help some of them through periods of financial difficulty, but certainly partly also deliberately, in the interests of her collection, for from Bremmer she had learned the principle that one only really gets to know art by comparison. Thus works of differing quality, and also of different periods and stemming from different cultures, had to be represented in the collection. Mrs. Kröller wrote in 1933, 'It was the intention in forming the collection to show, to bring out the fact, that abstract art is not an insuperable obstacle, but that it has always existed. It is for this reason that you will find here new and old works side by side. I wanted through the old to substantiate the case of the new'. These old works are mainly 16th- and 17th-century paintings from the Netherlands, Flanders and Germany; no examples of Mannerism or flamboyant Baroque, but quiet, restrained compositions.

As far as comparison with other cultures was concerned, Hélène Kröller bought old Chinese, Japanese, Siamese and Javanese and ancient Egyptian and Greek sculpture and ceramics. In fact she was much interested in oriental art, one of the reasons being that it had been passed on through the centuries by the community. 'Art must be cultivated down the generations for centuries and centuries, before it reaches such a state of clarity as is revealed to us here', wrote Bremmer in connection with a Japanese Buddha in the collection.

Like the concept *Spiritus et Materia Unum,* this statement is a key to the ideal collection that Hélène Kröller envisaged – art that is cultivated by the community and 'revealed' in a state of clarity. The greater part of her art collection, because it was still so recent, would have to be cultivated by the community that came after her. Or: would it cultivate the community? She believed that was possible too. Wilhelm Worringer, who had made abstract art acceptable and enjoyable to many people with his *Abstraktion und Einfühlung* (1906), had written that art is always a reflection of the inner life of the artist, but that the spectator, too, forms the work of art. 'The form of an object is always the form that I endow it with, through my spiritual and mental activity. It is a fundamental fact of all psychology and, above all, precisely of all aesthetics, that an 'object perceivable by the senses' is of itself a non-object, something that does not and cannot exist. Because it exists for me – and there can be no question of any other kind of object – it is penetrated by my involvement with it, by my inner life.' Mrs. Kröller understood the possible consequence of this theory: art, or just an aesthetic experience, can also form the spectator.

In order to be able to give direction to the spiritual development of the community, she wanted her collection to be lucid, 'in a state of clarity', not only in content, but also in form. In the choice of the objects their aesthetic quality was her highest criterion. In handing over her collection to the State, she let it pass out of her hands, in her view, 'as a modern collection unique of its kind, because of its faultless structure and intrinsic value'. It was a stable unity that could certainly be extended, but not arbitrarily, and for that reason she wrote a memorandum which the State was intended to take as a directive after the transfer, particularly in questions of purchase and management.

Since then purchasing policy has been directed at keeping Mrs. Kröller's original collection, comprising painting and sculpture of the 19th and early 20th centuries, older European and Eastern Asiatic art, intact as a unit. That is to say, it can be amplified here and there with works by such artists as Cézanne or the Futurists, which fit into the collection as a whole or which we know Mrs. Kröller would have liked to have had, but to extend it with, for example, Expressionist or Surrealist paintings would disturb its balance and its character and this is, therefore, inadmissible. For these reasons the museum is precluded from ever endeavouring to give an art-historical survey in which all currents are represented. That is a limitation, but not a disadvantage, for it means that, along with the carefully chosen acquisitions, the collection retains a clear and definite form.

There are, however, changes in aspect, since the way we look at art and our evaluation of it alters in the course of time. There are paintings which Mrs. Kröller thought worth showing that now hang in the storeroom, but there are also others that can be exhibited with much more emphasis than before. For the rest, the vast majority of the works that Mrs. Kröller considered important are still also important for us today, although this may in part be for different reasons. With the idea *Spiritus et Materia Unum* in mind, Mrs. Kröller collected modern art that was in some cases so new and different that she and her contemporaries were thrown off balance by it. Our attitude to her collection is now quite different. *Spiritus et Materia Unum* is no longer actual for us and the shock effect of the art of that time has become part of history. Nevertheless, the primary demand Mrs. Kröller made of her purchases – that their aesthetic quality should be high enough – has ensured that her collection is also highly regarded today. This is also due in part to the fact that many of the artists whose work she bought have risen sharply in the general estimation in the last fifty years, not only because their significance for the development of art has become even clearer, but also because the publicity value of some of them has played a powerful role – to name a few names: Mondriaan, Léger, Picasso and, above all, Van Gogh, who has grown into an almost mythological figure.

One side of the policy of the museum at the present time is, therefore, to preserve the original Kröller-Müller collection and keep it alive. The other is concerned with the art of our own time and especially with contemporary sculpture. After the war Mrs. Kröller's modest collection of sculpture was extended, inspiration being derived here from the favourable spiritual climate that existed internationally at that time for the holding of exhibitions of sculpture (of which the best examples are the open-air exhibitions in London, Arnhem-Sonsbeek and Antwerp mentioned above). The growing collection of sculpture and sculptors' drawings (which were not necessarily studies or working drawings for pieces acquired) came more and more strongly to form the second core of the museum's activities alongside the Kröller-Müller collection. An abundance of space for these activities was provided by the opening of the sculpture garden behind the museum in 1961 and its extension in 1965, which also made it possible to achieve an optimal experience of the relationship between art and nature. Thus Dubuffet's *Jardin d'émail* (1974), a dazzling white artificial garden of concrete, affords a sharp contrast to the natural garden around it, while Serra's *Spin out* (1973) divides up the space in a recess in the low ridge round the sculpture park. Serra was himself invited to choose a place and design a project for it and that opportunity has been extended to others as well, such as Marta Pan, who made a floating sculpture for the pool in 1961, Rickey, the forms of whose *Two vertical and three horizontal lines* (1965–66) are constantly altered by the wind, and Van de Kop, who has completely altered the spatial impression of a grassy area by aligning his *Tûam* (1974) across its long axis. The re-erection in the sculpture park of the Rietveld Pavilion, which was designed in 1955 for a sculpture exhibition held that year in Sonsbeek Park, was made possible by friends of Rietveld as an act of homage to him and here nature, sculpture and architecture now come together. In addition, commissions were given to artists not only for sites in natural settings near the museum, but also for places inside the building itself, Van Elk, Ad Dekkers, Van Munster and Struycken making projects that took the architecture of the museum as their starting-point.

Between the modern art that Hélène Kröller collected and the contemporary art now being acquired by the museum there are enormous differences, for the changes in art over the last hundred years have been numerous and profound. But there is also a similarity nonetheless. Through the confrontation with important new artistic expressions we are again and again compelled 'to look at the old afresh, to fathom the new and to estimate both at their true value'.

Illustrations

Paintings   41
Drawings   102
Sculptures   116
Sculpture park   138

School of GIOVANNI DI PAOLO
(1403–c.1482, Italy)

The adoration of the Kings
panel, 43.5 × 47 cm

Mention has been made in the introduction to this book of Mrs. Kröller's theory that realism and also – less obviously – idealism (the abstract) appear in the art of all periods. In order to demonstrate this, she also bought European and non-European art of past ages. 'It was the intention in forming the collection to show, to bring out the fact, that abstract art is not an insuperable

obstacle, but that it has always existed. It is for this reason that you will find here *new* and *old* works side by side. I wanted through the old to substantiate the case of the new'.

In this little painting by a pupil of Giovanni di Paolo we find the abstract and reality in combination. Two episodes are recounted in the composition: in the top half the three kings from the east (note the camels and the monkey) accompanied by their train, come riding towards us through the mountains, led by the star: in the following scene, in the bottom half of the

picture, they have arrived at the stable in Bethlehem to adore the Child. The star has also moved and now shines above the stable. The mountains, the trees, the stony ground and the city are strongly stylized, but the figures are painted as realistically as possible, with anecdotal details. There is no perspective and the figures in the foreground and background are virtually the same size. One could make a comparison here with the early Cubist landscapes of Picasso and Braque, who deliberately abandoned perspective.

BARTHEL BRUYN THE ELDER
(c.1492–1555, Germany)

Portrait of the wife of Gerhard (or Arnold) von Westerburg
panel, 61 × 51 cm, 1524

This early 16th-century portrait is the companion piece to a portrait in the Kunsthistorisches Museum in Vienna, which is probably of Gerard von Westerburg, an adherent of the Reformation. He married Jena Gertraude von Leutz, the woman in this portrait, in 1523. We may take it that Bruyn has painted her as faithfully as possible, but in accordance with the custom of the time he has also added an attribute, namely the pink, which had the significance of a pure and living love and was at the same time a reminder of the Passion of Christ. On the back of the portrait still more symbols appear, those of *Vanitas*, the transitoriness of all earthly things. There we find death in the form of a skull, a fly (decomposition and decay) and a snuffed candle accompanied by a saying in Latin, which may be translated as: 'Everything is predestined to disappear: death is the end of things'. This saying can be called Humanistic rather than Christian. At all events it reveals an uncertainty about a life after death. Thus it is the material and the earthly that is emphasised in this portrait. The painter has devoted maximum attention to the richness of the costume and that was probably one of the few certainties that people had left in those turbulent times, when everything had been cut adrift from the old moorings – both the church and the universe of which the earth was no longer the centre. And in fact the saying comes, not from a Christian author, but from the Roman poet Lucretius. The portrait stems from the climate of Humanism, in which attention was focused completely on man, on the individual, provided, of course, that he was of some significance, for whatever reason.

FLORIS VAN SCHOOTEN
(before 1612–after 1655, Netherlands)

Breakfast piece
panel, 47 × 84 cm

This extremely realistic 17th-century still life affords an opportunity for comparison with the 19th- and 20th-century still lifes in the Kröller-Müller collection. Such a comparison is, as far as the 19th-century is concerned, an obvious one, since so many painters of that time (Allebé, Fantin Latour, Bonvin and numerous others) drew inspiration for their still lifes from the art of our Golden Age. The prosperity of that period brought painters closer to matter, to the material. While a still life of, say, a set table with bread, wine and fruit may appear in the 15th and 16th centuries in portraits or religious scenes as a *memento mori* or symbol of the Eucharist, in this painting by Floris van Schooten the still life has become an independent subject, in which the transitoriness of earthly things is pointed out, albeit in veiled terms. The warning is scarcely a strong one, for the emphasis in this breakfast falls on abundance, an abundance recorded with a photographic accuracy. That abundance was due in those days to the trade with the Far East, of which the Chinese plate is a reminder.

Floris van Schooten worked in Haarlem between 1612 and 1655. He painted a great many breakfast pieces which are characterized by great simplicity. Notwithstanding the copious eatables, there are no goblets or silver vessels of an overdone beauty here, as there are in, for example, the still lifes of Heda, a contemporary of Van Schooten. This quiet simplicity will perhaps have been one of Mrs. Kröller's reasons for buying this picture. It was this quietness that she also found in the still lifes of Fantin Latour (see p.45).

JEAN BAPTISTE CAMILLE COROT
(1796–1875, France)

View of Soissons
canvas, 80 × 100 cm, 1833

Although Corot was a 19th-century painter, his work seems to be more closely
linked with the Classicism of French and
Italian painting of the 17th and 18th
centuries. In it one can find the strength of
composition of Poussin's landscapes and the
lightness and poetry of Watteau's *Fêtes
champêtres*.

This painting was made in 1833 to a
commission from the draper Henry who
could see this view from the window of his
office. The spectator is led into the painting
in a traditional manner: in the foreground
are flowers and bushes accurately rendered
in dark brownish-green tones, while the
girl and the reclining boy supply the then
well-nigh obligatory figure interest, the
'animation' of the landscape. Via the
diagonal line of the Abbey of St. Jean des
Vignes one arrives at a sunlit stretch of
countryside with the cathedral of Soissons

on the horizon. In contrast to the foreground this area is painted much more
sketchily in the light greyish-green tone
that is so characteristic of Corot.

The light is a highly essential element
here. The cloudy sky and rather low horizon relate the painting to Dutch 17th-
century landscapes, which began to be
admired again in the last century. The
bright light and the ethereal, hazy forms in
Corot's later paintings made their mark on
the young Impressionists.

HENRI JEAN THÉODORE FANTIN LATOUR
(1863–1904, France)

Still life
canvas, 73 × 58 cm, 1866

'Painting is in essence completely concrete and can only consist of the depiction of things that really exist. An abstract object, which cannot be seen and does not exist, does not belong in the realm of painting'. Thus wrote Courbet in 1861 to the students, or, as he termed them, assistants, at his open, undogmatic and democratic studio. Among them was Fantin Latour, who in his lifetime painted a great many still lifes, often with flowers, fruit and pottery. Courbet's pronouncement is quoted here because Fantin Latour abided by it in his still lifes. He painted existing objects quite simply and straightforwardly and the results are reminiscent of the still lifes of the Dutch 17th-century masters or of Chardin. But there is more to it than that: the dark background, the way the objects are composed on the white tablecloth and the subdued colours give this still life a quietude and gravity that go beyond reality. In contrast to Courbet, Fantin saw in colour a poetry, 'which gives rise to thousands of things that the eye cannot see', and he compared this poetry to the power of music to stir the imagination.

This sort of stilled realism appealed to Mrs. Kröller more than that of Courbet and at one time she bought 16 paintings, some drawings and numerous lithographs by Fantin. She called this still life 'sublime'. For her it signified 'the quiet reverence towards every event'.

JEAN-FRANÇOIS MILLET
(1814–75, France)

Woman baking bread
canvas, 55 × 46 cm, 1854

Millet was born on a farm on the coast near Gruchy in Normandy. He grew up in the country and remained linked with it at the little village of Barbizon in the wooded environs of Fontainebleau, to which he moved in 1849 and where he lived until his death. There also lived many other painters who as a group acquired the name of Barbizon School, and who became known for their Realistic-Romantic vision of landscape. Millet, however, painted the peasants working on the land in the main. His subject matter may perhaps have been influenced to some extent by the revolution of 1848, but the rising socialism of those days was not the real source of his paintings. In his work he exalted the honest and simple life and work on the land, contrasting it with the lifestyle of the urban bourgeoisie. He painted the peasants as great heroic figures bound up with the earth. Often seen slightly from below, they completely dominate his canvases. His colours are subdued and harmonious and the contrasts of light and dark are concentrated on the figures, so that they emerge even more strongly. Millet's work had a great influence on the art of the 19th century. An obvious example of this is Van Gogh, who drew inspiration time and time again from Millet's paintings.

GUSTAVE COURBET
(1819–77, France)

Portrait of Madame Jolicler
(canvas, 44.5 × 37 cm, c.1872

Courbet was the leading light of Realism, the movement in art and literature that came strongly to the fore after the middle of the last century. For him realism, which has taken many forms in the history of modern art to date, was based on a completely straightforward premise, which he set out in the *Realistic Manifesto* (1855). What was revolutionary in his work was the simplicity and faithfulness to truth of his subjects. He painted people and their customs and ideas as an image of the times and he did this not only as an artist, but above all also as a man who was involved in the social and political events of his day. As a result of his active participation in the Commune of 1871 he was banished to Switzerland in 1873.

This portrait is not a typical example of his realism, but more of a document: the likeness – in profile, which is a rarity for him – of his faithful friend Lydie Marthe Chenoz (who married Charles Jolicler in 1863), who gave him her unfailing support and looked after his affairs during his exile in Switzerland. The painting is completely subdued in colour and Courbet has concentrated entirely on the profile of the face.

ADOLPHE JOSEPH MONTICELLI
(1824–86, France)

Flowerpiece
canvas, 52.5 × 33.5 cm, 1875

We are readily inclined to put artists into
clearly defined art-historical pigeon-
holes. It is easy and convenient to do so and
it also answers the common human need to
want to belong somewhere. But we must
not forget that every person is an individual who expresses himself in his own
way, which is never like that of another.
Monticelli was an artist who went his own
way more than anyone else. This finds
expression in, among other things, the
exceptional way he treated colour and
handled oil paint as a medium. In this
flowerpiece we see a method of painting
which was completely unusual for that
time. The forms of the flowers and the vase
are dissolved in the thick mass of paint, in
which only the colours reveal that what we
have here is a flowerpiece. Monticelli was
ignored in his own day. People thought, so
we learn from Van Gogh, that he was an
alcoholic and that that was why he painted
so strangely. Van Gogh, however, saw
what was exceptional in him and always
defended his work. He discerned something passionate and eternal in these paintings and had a great admiration for the way
in which Monticelli handled colour. He felt
a kinship with him. According to him,
Monticelli was able to paint so intensely
only because he deliberately went to the
limit both physically and spiritually. An
exceptional man, who is supposed to have
said, 'I come from the moon', when
someone asked him where he lived.

MATTHIJS MARIS
(1839–1917, Netherlands, France, England)

The spinster
canvas, 91 × 61 cm, 1873

Matthijs Maris is mostly mentioned in the same breath as his two brothers, Jacob and Willem, the landscape painters of the Hague School. But if his brothers found their inspiration in the then still unspoiled landscape around The Hague, of which they tried to represent the light and atmosphere as truly as possible, Matthijs' work is based on the dream, on an imaginary world, on the 'purely spiritual'. 'My paintings are the incomplete expressions of my thoughts; they belong to me, they are part of my soul and I alone understand them and appreciate how inadequate they are to express what is in me'. This longing to make his thoughts and feelings visible led Maris to produce romantic, mystical scenes in which historical architecture (castles) and costumes appear over and over again. He had an admiration for Leonardo da Vinci and Holbein, and also for the English climate of the Pre-Raphaelites (Rossetti and Burne-Jones) and German Romantic painters. In this painting, *The spinster,* the non-Dutch character becomes clear. Maris did it in 1873, when he was living in Paris, and he also made a related picture there, which is called *He is coming* and in which a young man appears in the background. In both scenes we can feel an inner longing for a dream world.

Maris fled away from hard reality, impelled by a vital need commonly felt at that time, which the Symbolists of a later period (such as Redon) were to translate into even more penetrating images.

PIERRE AUGUSTE RENOIR
(1841–1919, France)

The café
canvas, 35 × 28 cm, c.1876–77

Was it a chance concurrence of circumstances that it should have been precisely the photographer Nadar who opened his studio in 1874 for the first exhibition of the Impressionists? Photography, that 19th-century invention, came as a revelation to painters. They saw how the mechanical eye could observe and record reality and it is no wonder that many of them called on photography to aid them in their work. Renoir, too, aimed to get as close to reality as possible, but his paintings are far removed from photographs for all that. The eye he used for his observations was the human eye, not the mechanical one, and those observations penetrated beyond the mere forms. Light, colour, movement, atmosphere, the vibration of the air and, one might say, everything that stimulates the senses was taken in and set down. This little painting is a splendid example of this.

In contrast to a photograph everything here is unsharp. There are no clear outlines. Everything is in movement. Everything is given form by means of colour, colours which here and there have been applied in layers one on top of the other. It is a refined play of contrasts. In some places Renoir has worked rapidly (*e.g.* the figures in the mirror), in others he has set the colour down with a great deal of deliberation (the two women). The result is an extremely lively snapshot of the carefree life of Fin de Siècle Paris, a life reserved only for a few, which held so much fascination for Renoir.

JOHAN BARTHOLD JONGKIND
(1819–91, Netherlands, France)

Fishing boat on the beach
canvas, 41.5 × 56 cm, 1861

The encouragement Jongkind received in Holland around 1840 did not mean that people there were prepared to go along with his later development. On the contrary, it was in France that his work found admirers. Pissarro said of him, 'If he had never existed, we (the Impressionists) would not be here either'. Monet regarded himself as Jongkind's pupil when he was with him daily in Honfleur around 1864, and Manet called him 'the father of the landscape painters'. In 1860 ninety French artists, including Corot, Daubigny and Millet, each sent a painting to a sale, the proceeds of which were to enable Jongkind to return to Paris again after a lonely period of five years in the Netherlands.

Jongkind painted this boat in 1861 and there is still something Dutch about it, which may be compared to the work of the later Hague School painters. However, there are also essential differences. This painting is empty, still and entirely considered in composition. The brownish colour of the sketchily painted boat and the fishwife provides a contrast to the soft, bright blue that dominates the rest of the canvas. The painting is more of a study in blue than a realistic beach scene such as is to be found later in the work of Mesdag, for example. This stating of problems of colour and light found more response among French painters than Dutch at that time.

CLAUDE MONET
(1840–1926, France)

The artist's boat
canvas, 50 × 64 cm, c.1874

In 1874 a group of young French painters
exhibited their work in the studio of the
photographer Nadar in Paris. Among them
was Monet, who showed twelve paintings,
including *Impression, soleil levant* from which
the journalist Leroy coined a derisory name
for the group, *Impressionists*. It is practically
impossible now for us to believe that the
paintings of these artists could have aroused
so much opposition and revulsion at that

time, although that vehement criticism is
strongly reminiscent of the cries of
'rubbish' we still hear so often nowadays.
Their work was diametrically opposed to
the highly esteemed historical and alle-
gorical subjects of the day, which were
painted with an almost photographic
accuracy in the artist's studio. The Impressionists, by contrast, left their studios
to paint in the open air, in the midst of
nature, their palette becoming lighter as a
result. They limited their subject matter to
the observed reality of, for example, a
landscape, preferably with the water of a
river or lake. In fact, however, the theme

itself was not so important to them. What
they were concerned with were the imma-
terial aspects: the light out of doors, the
movement of air and water, the fleeting
moment. In this painting by Monet we can
see that the forms are not clearly outlined;
they are created by means of the colour
contrasts painted in short, rapid touches.
Monet painted the boat he used as a studio
on the Seine near Argenteuil, thereby
making a statement that established the
credo and method of work to which he
was to remain faithful all his life.

PIERRE AUGUSTE RENOIR
(1841–1919, France)

The clown

canvas, 193.5 × 130 cm, 1868

In Renoir's work we find few landscapes – the favourite subject of the Impressionists – but quantities of portraits, nudes and scenes from the light-hearted life of La Belle Epoque. In his youth he was already in the habit of drawing and painting people in cafés and he probably also got portrait commissions as a result of this. At all events he painted this clown at the request of the owner of the café of the Cirque d'Hiver in Paris, who may possibly have wanted to have the picture in his establishment as an advertisement for the circus, but who never actually gained possession of it as he was unable to pay the fee. The clown is John Price, a well-known artist at that time. He and his brother William appeared as musician-clowns in costumes decorated with butterflies.

The painting dates from Renoir's early period, when he made large, detailed portraits which often fill the entire canvas. Here too he has concentrated on the figure of the clown, who is shown at more than life size against the ochre colour of the sand. The white chair and the white edge of the ring contrast sharply with the otherwise dark tones. The clown is portrayed with precision, but the spectators are painted much more sketchily in dark greys, so that they remain vague figures in the background.

PAUL GAUGUIN
(1848–1903, France, Tahiti)

The edge of the wood
canvas, 81 × 64.5 cm, 1885

Gauguin began painting relatively late. He worked first as a merchant seaman and later as a stockbroker on the Paris exchange. He was incited by friends to take up drawing and painting in 1871 and he began to get more and more interested in art, even buying a number of Impressionist paintings in 1876. The following year he had a great deal of contact with Pissarro, who gave him advice on painting and urged him to participate in the exhibitions of the Impressionists. From 1883 on he devoted himself entirely to his art, to the great distress of his wife who felt that this choice meant the end of the prosperity in which the Gauguin family had lived up to then. In 1885 Gauguin left his family to live on his own in Paris – this picture was painted in that year. At first sight the landscape looks Impressionistic, but when one looks at it more closely the colours, the brushwork and the composition prove to possess a dreamy character which is introspective rather than focused on reality.

What Gauguin has painted here is his inner experience of this landscape. In a letter of that year he speaks of human feelings and sensations which cannot be put into words, but which the artist can translate with the aid of colour and line. In this painting can be seen the beginning of his later work, in which the emotional values of colour took on a symbolic significance.

PAUL CÉZANNE
(1839–1906, France)

The road beside the lake

canvas, 92 × 75 cm, c.1885–90

Like Symbolism, the work of Cézanne is a
reaction against the changing representation of visible reality of the Impressionists, who let their brushes be guided by
the eye alone. Cézanne used the intellect as
well as visual sensations in his work,
arranging, systematizing and searching for a
firmer foundation for painting. He realised
that art has a reality of its own, which is
'apprehended with the eyes'. He tried to
find an underlying system in nature, but
although he saw in nature a number of
basic forms, the sphere, the cylinder and the
cone, his work was not based on form but
on colour, since, in his view, form and its
volume are contained in the contrasts and
relationships between colours and tones
(light/dark). According to him, there are no
lines or volumes, but only contrasts. This
starting-point of Cézanne's implied an ob-
jectivization of reality, which also came to
the fore, although in a different way, in
Seurat and which was to lead to the analysis
of forms in space of Cubism and the abstraction of the later Constructivist movements in modern painting.

   In this painting we can see in the first
instance that Cézanne has set down his
brush strokes in three directions: vertical,
horizontal and diagonal (towards one side
only). With this he has excluded his own,
sensitive 'handwriting' (*cf.* Seurat). In
addition he has, indeed, worked with
colour contrasts: various tones of ochre,
green, grey, blue and white, whereby the
forms (strong and without detail) are
created.

GEORGE HENDRIK BREITNER
(1857–1923, Netherlands)

The gust of wind
canvas, 24 × 35 cm, c.1890

There are many factors that determine an artist's life and work, such as, for example, his milieu and surroundings and the time in which he lives. In the case of Breitner the city and the Dutch climate clearly came into play. He has been called one of the Amsterdam Impressionists, but how different his Impressionism is from that of his contemporaries. He opted for grey, rainy weather, snow, wind and the dark days of autumn and winter when people hurry through the streets.

This little painting is a snapshot, a sketch set down rapidly and without hesitation in order to catch the atmosphere of the moment as well as possible. Breitner wandered around the streets of Amsterdam armed with his sketchbook and camera to capture the life of the city and transcribe it in his paintings. He discovered its exceptional beauty, which for him lay above all in the people who lived there.

At the end of the 19th century Amsterdam expanded into a large city. There was a tremendous amount of building going on and this held an enormous fascination for Breitner, albeit he liked the old Amsterdam better than the new. His paintings of piledriving, demolition work, horses, workmen and women in the streets reveal the dynamism and restlessness of this urge for urban renewal. He himself was also of a restless and emotional character, always on the look out for deep, vivid experiences, but never entirely satisfied with them. There is no optimism in his work, nor in this painting either, but rather a feeling of uncertainty about the future, about the new age that was already visible.

FLORIS VERSTER
(1861–1927, Netherlands)

Still life
panel, 17 × 25.5 cm, 1914

When Verster painted this still life in 1914, Mondriaan had already been engaged on his abstract compositions for some time. Mrs. Kröller bought this picture in 1915 and in the same year she also acquired Mondriaan's *Composition No. 10* for her collection.

Although Verster's painting comes very close to reality, there is also something abstract about it, *i.e.* there is more there than what you can see. In the pure forms of the eggs and the wooden bowl, in the contrast between light and dark and in the way in which he has concentrated completely on the objects, Verster has managed to summon into being a tension that is endowed with something fundamental. As the poet Verwey put it: 'The eye saw as if in a dream yet it looked closely'. In that

sense this still life may be compared with that by Fantin Latour (see p.45). There is a story to the effect that Verster sometimes painted his still lifes with his back to the objects, completely concentrating on his work and undistracted by reality. Here he has isolated the bowl of eggs from everyday reality, separating it, as it were, from its functional value. He painted many of his still lifes in a wholly restrained and quiet manner, focusing all his attention on the materiality of the things.

PAUL JOSEPH CONSTANTIN GABRIEL
(1828–1903, Netherlands)

Train in a landscape (il vient de loin)
canvas, 67 × 100 cm, c.1887

The subject is a simple one: the flat, wide polderland with its waters and vapours. The picture is painted in carefully considered tones of grey and green and the strong perspective immediately draws us straight into the middle of the landscape. Something out of the ordinary is going on: coming towards us is a train that will

gradually break the silence. This is one of the few paintings, if not the only one, in Dutch art of that period in which the 'new age' is treated in such a subtle, yet penetrating way. Before Gabriel, Monet and Turner had also painted this prosaic machine that disturbs the beauty of the landscape. Gabriel was a realist who turned his back on any representation or feeling that was not grounded in reality. He did not like the beautiful 'greys' of painters like Mauve or the Maris brothers, but saw the Dutch landscape, by contrast, as rich, lush and full of colour. This painting was done

around 1887 shortly after he returned to Holland after a period of 24 years in Belgium. Perhaps that was why his view of the flat polderland was so clear and direct.

Mrs. Kröller bought this Gabriel in 1907 when she had just begun to follow Bremmer's lessons and start collecting. The simplicity and clarity that distinguish her collection already appealed to her then in this painting. She herself wrote of 'Gabriel's spirit, his individuality, his personality, that comes out of this work to meet you'.

VINCENT VAN GOGH
(1853–90, Netherlands, France)

Young girl in a wood
canvas, 39 × 59 cm, September 1882

All Van Gogh's work is characterized by a highly personal, emotional and often visionary approach to the reality of his immediate surroundings. That may be true of many artists, but the intensity of Van Gogh's work as the precipitation of his life and thoughts, about which we know so much from his letters to his brother Theo, is exceptional for the period in which he lived and for our own time too. Even before he became aware in 1880 of his vocation to become a painter, he had an eventful life behind him in which art and religion were the essential factors that were to determine his future course.

This painting of a girl in a wood was made in 1882, at the time when Van Gogh was living in The Hague and had begun, under Mauve, to paint in oils. The dour power of his figure drawings of that year – of old men and women and of Sien and her child, whom he had taken into his own home – is also to be found here in spite of the problems of the new technique and '…the great difficulty of keeping it clear…of making it so that people can breathe in it and walk through it and smell the wood'. Van Gogh wanted to reproduce the autumn atmosphere as faithfully as possible, even taking a bit of earth back to his studio for the purpose. The subject comes from one of the English prints he collected. Its title, *Innocent*, has an emotional value which he may also have wanted to put into the painting. In a comparable way he gave a nude study of Sien of the same year the title *Sorrow*.

VINCENT VAN GOGH
(1853–90, Netherlands, France)

Loom and weaver
canvas, 70 × 85 cm, May 1884

In September 1883 Van Gogh went from
The Hague to Drenthe, where he was
powerfully affected by the lonely landscape
and the poor peasant population who lived
there in difficult circumstances. Although
he described the atmospheric landscape in
detail in his letters, in his work he concentrated more on the people and their work
and the way in which they lived. This
interest becomes even clearer in the period

he spent with his parents at Nuenen
(December 1883–November 1885), where he
painted men and women working on the
land and weavers. The Nuenen period was
a very fruitful one and his work became
more sure in form and acquired greater
clarity. His colour remained dark and it was
also tone (contrasts between light and dark)
that he was more concerned with.

There are many versions of the *Weaver.*
These men behind their looms, who
worked all day long in low, dark rooms,
intrigued Van Gogh. He made the mecha-
nism into something human, an extension
of the weaver who 'ought to be the *heart*

of it and achieved with the most feeling,
the rest being kept subordinate to him.
Sometimes a sort of sigh or lamentation
must come out of that jumble of laths'.

Van Gogh wanted to bring this existence
to life. He wanted to be a painter of that
peasant life in which he was so intensely
wrapped up that, as he wrote, he no longer
thought of anything else. His great model
was Millet (see also p.46), whom he called
at that time: '*Father Millet,* counsellor and
leader in everything for the younger
painters'.

VINCENT VAN GOGH
(1853–90, Netherlands, France)

Birds' nests
canvas, 33.5 × 50.5 cm, October 1885

In the last months that he spent at Nuenen Van Gogh made five paintings of birds' nests. In his youth he had already made collections of plants and animals that he found on his rambles through the country-side, and a friend of his from Eindhoven, in recalling later on what his studio at Nuenen was like, mentioned 'a cupboard with as many as thirty different birds' nests and all sorts of mosses and plants brought back from the heath'. Vincent wrote to Theo in early October 1885 that he was working on these paintings and that he hoped that 'through the colours of the moss, withered leaves and grasses, clay, etc. they might succeed in pleasing some people who have a good knowledge of nature'. He painted them on a black background 'for the reason that I want it to come out plainly in these studies that the objects are not in their natural settings, but on a conventional background'. He also sent a basket of nests to the painter Van Rappard: 'I thought that you, like me, might perhaps take pleasure in the birds' nests, since birds like the wren or the golden oriole can really and truly also be ranked among artists. The nests are nice for still lifes too'.

In the letter to Theo he added as a foot-note: 'In the work of Millet and Lhermitte all reality is also a symbol at the same time', and that these nests likewise had a deeper significance for him is also shown by the words he wrote under a little pen sketch of a nest in the letter: 'As the winter draws on and I have got time for it I shall make some drawings of things of this sort. *La nichée et les nids,* that's what I have a heart for – especially the *human* nests, those cottages on the heath and their inhabitants'.

VINCENT VAN GOGH
(1853–90, Netherlands, France)

The potato eaters
canvas on panel, 72 × 93 cm, April 1885

For Van Gogh the painting of the potato eaters was the most important picture he made in Nuenen and it is perhaps because of that that it became so well-known. He prepared the subject in detail, making separate studies of the figures and of the composition as a whole. This painting is the last study before the final canvas which now hangs in the Van Gogh Museum in Amsterdam. Van Gogh wrote about it at length in his letters to Theo. Here again Millet was his model, the painter who entered into the life of the peasants, who was satisfied '...in the matters of eating, drinking, clothes and sleeping with what the peasants were satisfied with...that made it that in my eyes he showed painters a way *as a human being...* No, one must paint the peasants as being oneself one of them'.

Van Gogh deliberately painted these people in 'their roughness', shunning any refinement of technique. 'I wanted it to make people think of quite a different way of life from that of us cultured people. This I would by no means want everyone just to regard it as beautiful or good'. He even tried to convey the character of this peasant life in the colour, using '...roughly the colour of a good earthy potato, naturally with its peel still on'. Here too he was thinking of Millet, whose peasants seem to be painted with the earth they are working. He used this indeterminate colour in light and dark tones trying to maintain clarity in the dark parts. Van Gogh captures the greyness of peasant life here. He painted the last version from memory, in order to achieve an even greater intensity.

VINCENT VAN GOGH
(1853–90, Netherlands, France)

Le Moulin de la Galette
canvas, 38.5 × 46 cm, spring 1886

In November 1885 Van Gogh left Nuenen and went to Antwerp to work at the Academy there. In Antwerp he saw the work of Rubens, which made a great impression on him and influenced his figure studies. It was there too that he got to know the art of the Japanese print, which was to be of great importance for his work in the years thereafter. In February 1886 he went to Paris. That city came as a revelation to him, for there he saw the art about which he had heard, read and himself written so much, that of Delacroix, Millet, Daumier, Monticelli and many others. He also got to know the work of younger artists there, the Impressionists, Cézanne, Seurat and Gauguin. Via the art-dealing businesses of his brother, Durand Ruel and Père Tanguy and at Cormon's studio, where he worked for a short time, he came into contact with many artists and made friends with a number of them.

In the first months he still kept to the dark colours he had used at Nuenen, although they are much less heavy, brighter and with sudden accents of colour, as in this painting of the Moulin de la Galette in Montmartre, near where he and his brother lived. He wandered round this neighbourhood a great deal, exploring his new surroundings with an openness to everything he saw about him, but without immediately accepting it. Through all changes of place and mood he remained himself, but 'the French air clears one's head and does one good – it's a world full of good things'.

VINCENT VAN GOGH
(1853–90, Netherlands, France)

Grassland
canvas, 31.5 × 40.5 cm, spring 1887

This little picture of grass, which Van Gogh probably painted in the spring of 1887, again illustrates his interest in nature, which extended from the earth to the starry sky. From his youth onwards he felt a bond with the earth and everything that lived on it. As we have already seen, he collected birds' nests, mosses and leaves, while the descriptions of the Drenthe landscape in his letters of 1883 are among the most beautiful passages in his correspondence. In Paris he painted crocuses that had just emerged from the ground. 'In every human being who is healthy and natural there is a *germinal power* like that of a grain of wheat. Thus the natural life is *germination*', he wrote to his sister in 1887. It was the life in nature that he always compared to man's existence, to his own life.

In painting this grass he will probably have been thinking of Japanese art where great attention is often given to grasses and undergrowth. In addition, he also knew the work of the painter Angrand, where comparable grassland can be found (albeit as part of a landscape). There are similarities in the style of painting, too, both artists arriving thereby at their own interpretation of Seurat's Divisionism. By a lively admixture of colour contrasts (green-red-pink and blue-yellow-orange with white) Van Gogh achieves in his grassland the vibration that hangs over a grassy meadow on a summer's day.

VINCENT VAN GOGH
(1853–90, Netherlands, France)

Interior of a restaurant
canvas, 54.5 × 56.5 cm, summer 1887

Van Gogh had already heard a great deal about Impressionism from Theo while still in Nuenen. In Paris he came into direct contact with it and made a thorough study of its colour theories which were new to him. This he had every opportunity of doing at the last Impressionist Exhibition in 1886, where, in addition, he saw Seurat's *La Grande Jatte*, painted in the stippled technique known as Divisionism. In 1886 and 1887 he himself experimented in numerous flower pieces 'in order to get used to other colours than grey, *i.e.* pink, soft or bright green, light blue, violet, yellow, orange, beautiful red'. He learned a lot from Pissarro, who explained the theories of the Impressionists and Seurat to him and who soon discovered his potentialities. Later, in the summer of 1887, he also came into contact with Signac, who propagated Divisionism more passionately than Pissarro. Although this contact led Van Gogh to make use of Divisionism, he handled it more spontaneously and more under the influence of immediate impulses. More-over he also understood that these theories and the technique would soon become fossilized as dogma. For the rest, he had a great admiration for Seurat, describing him later in Arles as 'le chef du petit Boulevard', the leader.

In this painting of a restaurant, which may be 'Chez bataille' where he and Theo regularly ate, we see how Van Gogh applied Divisionism in a fairly arbitrary and unconstrained way, combined with broad, full brush strokes, achieving an airy atmosphere with the stippled touches. In its colour scheme, too, this painting is freer, more Impressionistic.

VINCENT VAN GOGH
(1853–90, Netherlands, France)

Self portrait
oils on paper, 32 × 23 cm, autumn 1887

Van Gogh painted the majority of the more than twenty self portraits known to us during the two years that he lived in Paris. For him the painting of people, figures and portraits always came before landscape. 'The *portrait,* one can say of it that it is something old, but it is also completely new... I still always have hopes that a fine revolution is waiting for us in the portrait'.

Van Gogh painted himself in default of anyone else who was willing to sit for him, but also out of a need for self-examination. In his letters he often gives a description of his appearance; conversely he wrote to Theo at a certain point: 'I am even inclined to believe that the portrait can tell you better than the letter how things are going with me'. The series of portraits made in Antwerp and Paris show how his face changed. It is not only through the ever brighter colours that his face becomes ever more open, more honest and devoid of any attempt to create a better impression. He is inexorable towards himself. How he saw himself we can now see: he managed to penetrate to the remotest depths with his eyes.

This self portrait from the autumn of 1887 shows how he was working at that time with an abundance of complementary colours applied to the canvas with rapid brush strokes such as, for example, the Impressionist Pissarro used. The English painter Hartrick related how Van Gogh 'rolled his eyes and hissed sharply through his teeth when he uttered the words "blue", "orange" – complementary colours, of course'. That obsession also comes through in this portrait.

VINCENT VAN GOGH
(1853–90, Netherlands, France)

View of Saintes-Maries
canvas, 64 × 53 cm, June 1888

In the summer of 1887 Van Gogh was
already writing to his brother, 'And then I
shall retire to somewhere in the south so as
not to see so many painters, who repel me
as people', and in another letter he added,
'…where there is still more colour and still
more sun'. In February 1888 he moved to
Arles in Provence. He felt ill and withdrew
into himself 'without yet daring to hope',
but slowly and with fluctuating moods he
recovered, comforted by nature and the
southern climate. In the middle of June he
went for a week to Saintes-Maries on the
Mediterranean not far from Arles. There
he painted fishing boats on the beach and
this powerful picture with a view of the
little town. Everything he now saw in the
south he translated into and described in
colour: '…the sea of a very deep ultra-
marine, the beach of a purplish and pale
reddish colour as it seemed to me, with
bushes on the dunes… Prussian blue bushes'.
At the same period he wrote, 'I must
achieve a sureness of colour', and that he
did in this painting, in which the power and
intensity of the colour determine the
solidity of the forms. The colour contrasts
are varied in numerous ways in a great
many nuances of red, green, blue and
yellow tones, applied to the canvas in areas
and, in the foreground, rapid brush strokes.

VINCENT VAN GOGH
(1853–90, Netherlands, France)

Haystacks in Provence
canvas, 73 × 92.5 cm, June 1888

On 12 June Van Gogh wrote to his brother that he was going to make a painting of a farm with haystacks as a companion piece to his *Harvest* (now in the Van Gogh Museum, Amsterdam), a painting influenced by reminiscences of Cézanne. In the same letter he wrote that it was now quite different in the south from what it had been in the spring, '...but I certainly feel no

less love for the nature there that from now on begins to look burnt up. Everywhere now you see the colour of old gold, of bronze even more than copper, and that with the azure green of the white-hot sky. It has a lovely, extremely harmonious colour, with Delacroix-like broken tones'. It was on the basis of this vision of the summer landscape around Arles that Van Gogh painted these haystacks and he may perhaps also have had Monet's famous painting of the same subject in mind *(Impression, soleil levant)*. In connection with the then current Monet exhibition at

Boussod, Valadon & Cie, where Theo worked, Van Gogh wrote that he was very sorry not to be able to see the exhibition, but that he was seeing so much in the nature around him – especially now that harvesting was in progress – that he really could not think of anything else. In this painting he employed free, here and there whirling, brush strokes, which are less sure than in the *View of Saintes-Maries*. This intense, emotional handwriting and the bright colour, in which yellow predominates, convey his inner experience of his first summer in the south.

VINCENT VAN GOGH
(1853–90, Netherlands, France)

Café terrace by evening
canvas, 81 × 65.5 cm, September 1888

Van Gogh made this painting in the
autumn of 1888, when Paris was already far
behind him and he had developed his own
style of painting. 'I note that what I learned
in Paris has evaporated and that I have
returned to the ideas that came to me in the
country, before I knew the Impressionists'.
He worked rapidly and intensely, almost in
a trance and the colours and lines acquired a
greater tension. He wrote to his sister
Wilhelmien about this painting in great
detail: 'On the terrace there are little figures
of people who are drinking something. A
great yellow lamp lights up the terrace, the
front of the café, and the pavement and
even shines on the cobbles of the street,
which have a violet-pink colour. The
fronts of the houses on the street, which
runs into the distance under a sky strewn
with stars, are deep blue or violet with a
green tree. So there you are, an evening
scene without black, but only beautiful
blue, violet and green, and in this setting
the lit square is coloured sickly pale, lemon-
green. It gives me a very great deal of
pleasure to paint the evening on the spot. In
the past people made drawings and painted
the picture by day from the drawing, but to
me it seems exactly right to paint the thing
directly. It is true that I may mistake dark
blue for green, lilac-blue for lilac-pink,
because it is no longer possible to distinguish the quality of the tone, but it is the
only way to get away from our conventional evening with its poor, ashen, whitish
light. After all now, a simple candle already
gives us truly rich yellows and oranges'.

VINCENT VAN GOGH
(1853–90, Netherlands, France)

Pollard willows with setting sun
canvas, 31.5 × 34.5 cm, autumn 1888

One of the reasons why Van Gogh worked quickly, as he himself repeatedly pointed out, is that he wanted to convey in his paintings the tension he felt on seeing and experiencing, for example, a landscape, without letting himself be distracted by the technique of painting. That tension in him seems to lie between heaven and earth, between a strong bond with reality and at the same time with the metaphysical, with what lies beyond reality. He felt a similar tension in Japanese art, in which he had always had a great interest. On arriving in Arles he wrote to Theo, 'I have the feeling of being in Japan', and later, 'the Japanese draws quickly, very quickly, like lightning: his nerves are finer, his feelings simpler'.

At the same time as he did this landscape Van Gogh also painted a self portrait in which he depicted himself as a Japanese, as a 'devotee of the eternal Buddha'. He dedicated the portrait to Gauguin, who was to come to Arles in October. In the months before that he worked like one possessed and was virtually strained to breaking-point. It was at this period that this little picture was painted. Thanks to the bright, tense colour, as well as the deliberately sought for primitive forms (especially in the sun) and the rough, rapidly set down brush strokes, the landscape has a tragic power. 'Instead of trying to reproduce accurately what is before my eyes, I make a more arbitrary use of colour, in order to express myself forcefully'.

VINCENT VAN GOGH
(1853–90, Netherlands, France)

La Berceuse
canvas, 92 × 73 cm, December 1888–March 1889

In September 1888 Van Gogh moved into the 'yellow house' in Arles, which he hoped would become a centre for artists. He invited Gauguin to be the first to come and live with him there and in October Gauguin came. Van Gogh had a great admiration for him, attaching a great deal of importance to his opinion of his own paintings. However, the two artists were very different in their temperaments and interests and serious tensions arose between them, which reached a peak in December, when Van Gogh cut one of his ears off and was taken into hospital in a completely overwrought state, while Gauguin went back to Paris.

Van Gogh made five almost identical versions of this portrait of Madame Roulin (she and her husband had helped him as much as they could at this time) between December 1888 and March 1889. The simplification of colour and line (areas of even colour inside heavy outlines) was, like the decorative background, taken over from Gauguin. Earlier on, from August 1888, Van Gogh had already shown his admiration for Gauguin in this way in several portraits (*e.g.* of Roulin). He called this simplification abstraction, but gave it up as being too easy.

The title *Berceuse* was inspired by Pierre Loti's novel *Pêcheur d'Islande,* which describes how fishermen, alone at sea and exposed to every kind of danger, had a picture of a female figure in their cabin, which gave them, 'children and martyrs at the same time', a rocking feeling that reminded them of their own cradle songs. The title also relates to Van Gogh's own situation at this time when he felt himself lonely and abandoned.

VINCENT VAN GOGH
(1853–90, Netherlands, France)

Still life with drawing board and onions
canvas, 50 × 64 cm, January 1889

Gauguin's departure had been a severe disappointment to Van Gogh, '...precisely because it has upset everything, now that we had arranged and furnished the house so as to be able to put friends up there in times of difficulty'. The outburst of December had dealt him a heavy blow spiritually and mentally and as a result of Gauguin's going away his ideal of an artists' house had become an illusion. Although he went back home again in January, he was still suffering from being on his own. On 7 January he wrote to Theo, 'Tomorrow I am going to start work again. I shall begin with a still life or two in order to recover the habit of painting again'. He painted a crab lying on its back, a theme that has been regarded as a symbol of his own attempts to get back to normal life. This still life with onions was also done at that time. The objects that appear in it point to Van Gogh's situation at that moment: a letter from Theo, the book *Annuaire de la santé ou médecine et pharmacie domestiques* by F. V. Raspail, a man who had turned against official medicine, the sprouting onions on and beside a soup plate, a curative recommended by Raspail, the burning candle, a pitcher, a bottle of wine and his comforter – pipe and tobacco. The meaning of the painting lies in the struggle he was waging to recover from the shock and to forget the tensions of the time with Gauguin.

VINCENT VAN GOGH
(1853–90, Netherlands, France)

Cornfield with reaper and sun
canvas, 72 × 92 cm, June/September 1889

At the beginning of February 1889 Van Gogh again suffered a nervous breakdown. Shortly afterwards a number of inhabitants of Arles sent a petition to the mayor requesting that this dangerous lunatic be locked up. And for a short while he was indeed locked up, after which he was a broken man. It was made impossible for him to stay in Arles and he himself decided to move to the asylum of Saint-Paul de Mausole in St. Rémy, in order to be able to work there in peace. He went there in May 1889, his life thereafter being marked by widely fluctuating moods. Sometimes he had hallucinations and on occasions he was aggressive, but there were a lot of good times as well, in which he worked hard. He often sat in his room and he drew and painted the view from his window, a cornfield enclosed by a wall and with the mountains behind it, over and over again in all possible variations and in different lights and weather conditions. He began working on this golden yellow painting of the cornfield in June, but immediately afterwards he had a relapse and for two months he was unable to work. In September he went on with the painting, of which he made several versions. He wrote to Theo: 'The work is going fairly well – I'm struggling with a canvas that I had begun on several days before my indisposition, a reaper. The study is entirely yellow and terribly thickly painted, but the motif was beautiful and simple. At that time I saw in that reaper an indistinct figure slaving away like a devil in the blazing heat in order to get his work done – I saw in him an image of death in the sense that humanity is the corn that is being reaped. It is, therefore, – if you like – the opposite of that sower I made earlier on. But there is nothing sorrowful in this death. It takes place in broad daylight with the sun flooding everything with a beautiful golden light'.

VINCENT VAN GOGH
(1853–90, Netherlands, France)

Grass and tree trunks
canvas, 72 × 91 cm, April 1890

Just as he had been in Paris and Arles, so also in St. Rémy Van Gogh was preoccupied with undergrowth, flowers, plants, grasses and tree trunks, often grown over with ivy. Many of the works with these subjects were done in the park of the asylum. In addition to paintings, Van Gogh also made a number of fine drawings of these growing things, which he set down with the reed pen – which was little used at that time – perhaps again in imitation of the Japanese artists. In these drawings he used very varied hatchings, thick and thin lines, often curved, dots and a multitude of little, free, open circles and one can sometimes find similar structures in the paintings.

On 4 May he wrote to Theo: 'I have made two paintings of young grass in the park. One of them is very simple – you can see a quick sketch here – the trunk of a pine tree, violet-pink, and then the grass with white flowers and dandelions, a little rose-bush and other tree trunks in the background, at the top of the canvas'. He saw the earth, which is fertile and from which everything grows, as a source of power. There are some striking characteristics in this painting: the flowers and the grasses have a clear, regular structure and make a positive impression beside the tormented tree trunk in the foreground and the darker trunks at the top of the canvas. Van Gogh wrote at this time to his friend Bernard: 'I exaggerate, I sometimes change something in a motif, but in the last resort I never invent the whole painting. On the contrary, I find it all ready and waiting in nature, but it has to be extracted therefrom'.

VINCENT VAN GOGH
(1853–90, Netherlands, France)

Landscape with trees
canvas, 64 × 78 cm, July 1890

In May 1890 Vincent wrote to Theo: '…the surroundings here are beginning to weigh me down more than I can say – I have truly been patient for more than a year – I need air, I feel myself wasting away with sorrow and weariness. Now it is beginning to weigh on me so heavily here, I believe it is no more than fair that there should come an end of it'. He decided to go to Auvers sur Oise to the north of Paris. Pissarro had lived there and furthermore Dr. Paul Gachet was there, a physician with an interest in psychiatry, who himself painted and was very interested in art.

With some sadness Van Gogh left Provence in the middle of May and went to Auvers via Paris, where he visited Theo and his wife. In the two remaining months of his life he worked as if in a frenzy. In addition to drawings, he made 70 paintings, more than one a day on average. In this painting with the three trees the tensions seem to fan out towards more peaceful realms, while the lines of the earth have something of the character of running water, of rapids. '…If I should stop working, I might more quickly and easily lose what it has cost me so much to achieve. The prospects are becoming sombre. I see no happiness at all in the future.' On 29 July 1890 he found for himself the peace he had so often longed for.

MAURICE DENIS
(1870–1943, France)

April

canvas, 37.5 × 61 cm, 1892

Maurice Denis was the theoretician of the Nabis (the Prophets), a group of artists who had made it their aim to 'spiritualize' art – to represent what was in the imagination and not to copy from reality. They regarded Gauguin as their great predecessor, his search on the island of Tahiti for a new pure form and content for art serving them as their model. Gauguin rejected illusionistic perspective and modelling, painting colours inside outlines in areas which were rhythmically arranged.

We find the same thing in *April,* albeit less consistently carried through. The painting consists of filled in areas of which the edges become vaguer as they near the horizon. The whole effect is decorative, while the subject evinces the – often naïve – optimism which marks the Nabis and which in Denis was later transmuted into an exalted religiosity. The sinuous lines on the painting point to Art Nouveau, to which the Nabis contributed a great deal.

They did not limit themselves to painting either, but sought to integrate their art with architecture, the theatre and graphic design.

Denis' dictum: 'Remember that a painting – whether it shows a warhorse, a naked woman or some story or other – is essentially a flat plane on which the colours are arranged in a certain order', offered artists the possibility of working freely from their own imaginations. It is still quoted as a principle for abstract art.

ODILON REDON
(1840–1916, France)

The cyclops
panel, 64 × 51 cm, c.1895–1900

Against the emphasis laid by the Realists and Impressionists on the observation and depiction of visible reality there came a reaction in the form of Symbolism. The painters of the movement, such as Moreau and Redon, placed the accent precisely on the supernatural, the inexplicable, the dream and the vision. Here Redon has painted the Cyclops, a one-eyed giant borrowed also from Greek mythology. These stories of the world of the gods served artists from the Renaissance onwards as a permanent source of inspiration, a source that degenerated into cliché in the 19th century. With the Symbolists the tales acquired a new significance which was bound up with the essential function of mythology as a religious explanation of mysterious natural phenomena and the human psyche. At the period when Redon made this painting, Freud was also occupied with psychoanalysis.

The menace of the giant, or rather of the eye spying on the naked woman, is intensified by the unusually vivid colours Redon has used. He often represented the eye as an all-commanding being in its own right. For him it was the symbol of the perception of the mysterious, unknown inner life. One can understand why the Surrealists, the painters of what lays beyond reality, devoted so much attention to the work of this magician.

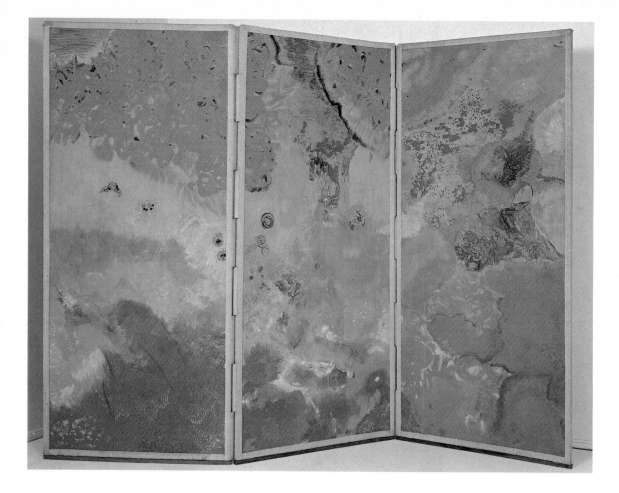

ODILON REDON
(1840–1916, France)

Three-fold screen with Pegasus
canvas, each section 173 × 78 cm, 1908

Through his friendship with Theo van Gogh André Bonger came into contact with the artistic world of Paris in the eighteen-eighties. One of his best friends was to be Odilon Redon whom he met for the first time in 1891, via the painter Émile Bernard. A year later, in 1892, Bonger went back to Holland and the friendship with Redon was further cemented by a long-lasting correspondence. In the autumn of 1906 Bonger asked Redon to make him a screen. After detailed discussion (by letter) about colour, proportions, dimensions and construction, the screen was finished in 1908. Redon wrote to Bonger at that time, 'The screen is ready at last... I believe it bears traces of the impressions I gained on my summer trip through the mountains. It is a sort of Chaos in the mountain tops, which can be seen through the amorphous beams of light. There are some cool blue-greys that I never use and that I must undoubtedly have brought back with me from my journey through Switzerland, stored away in my subconscious. Nothing comes about by chance'.

In this screen, Redon has depicted a being from Greek mythology, the winged horse Pegasus which, with its rider, Bellerophon, slew the Chimaera, a fire-breathing monster. There are no monsters here, only little embryonic winged creatures roaming about in the rarified sphere of colour. They come from Redon's imaginary world.

JAMES ENSOR
(1860–1949, Belgium)

The revenge of Hop-Frog
canvas, 114 × 81.5 cm, c.1910

In an acid, lollipop pink Ensor has here depicted the story by Edgar Allan Poe (based on one of Hans Andersen's fairy tales), in which the put-upon jester Hop-Frog took his revenge on his king and seven ministers by having them appear at a masked ball dressed as orangutans, hoisting them up on a chain and setting fire to them, while the masked revellers looked on. This harrowing image of spurious revelry, at which death is present and suddenly strikes, appears repeatedly in Ensor's work after 1888, in which he presents his fantasies about the evil powers of reality that disturb dreams. He is the pessimist who pictures the terrors of his time in his burlesques, just as Hieronymus Bosch, Breughel and Callot did in their days. His strange beings, his masks and pierrots, are also linked with Flemish popular theatre, where good and evil confront each other in all their intensity. For him life was a masquerade which tried in vain to conceal passion and brutality. The marvellously 'high-spirited', ethereal colours he uses make the contrast with his abrasive subjects all the greater, and he paints in a nervous manner, with short little strokes, drawing with the brush in the same way as he set the story of Hop-Frog on the etching-plate (1898).

The museum possesses six paintings by Ensor. His sarcastic and pitiless work falls rather outside the scheme of the Kröller-Müller collection, but it was Henry van de Velde who convinced Mrs. Kröller of Ensor's exceptional qualities.

GEORGE PIERRE SEURAT
(1859–91, France)

Honfleur harbour
canvas, 79.5 × 63 cm, 1886

In a letter written to a friend in 1890 Seurat set out a succinct definition of the basis on which he worked – a basis which, like the work of Cézanne, was to become one of the starting-points for the abstract art of this century. He wrote that for him art meant harmony and harmony signified the working in together of contrasts and similar elements, namely tone (light and dark), colour (each colour always with its complement from the spectrum: red/green, orange/blue, yellow/violet) and line (as direction). He also divided harmony into calm, gaiety or sadness. With calm there is a balance of tone and a balance between warm and cool colour and the line is horizontal. Gaiety implies light tone, warm colour and rising line, sadness dark tone, cool colour and falling line.

With this Seurat achieved an objective approach to reality, whereby he allowed his emotions to come into play as little as possible. By his use of the stipple technique he also excluded his own 'handwriting', mixing the colours in this way not on the palette, but – by optical means – through the eye of the spectator. He stylized reality and because of this his work is in essence abstract.

This painting of Honfleur is unfinished. Seurat only worked on the canvas for eight days and he thus regarded it as a large sketch. Nonetheless it is perfectly clear and it shows the first phase of his method of work, which is carried through to completion in *Le Chahut*. Seurat's work is a reaction against Impressionism, which he regarded as too emotional and not pure enough.

GEORGE PIERRE SEURAT
(1859–91, France)

Le Chahut
canvas, 169 × 139 cm, 1889–90

Seurat took the work of several theoreticians as his guide in his researches in the fields of tone, colour and line. *Le Chahut* evinces very clearly the aesthetic theories published around 1888 by the mathematician Charles Henry, who promulgated the scientific approach to the depiction of moods: gaiety, calm or sadness. In *Le Chahut* the gaiety of the dance predominates: the tone is light, the colours are warm, the lines and movements point upwards. Everything is in tune with the buoyant mood of the *café-chantant* with the exception of the darker tone and colour of the double-bass player in the foreground, with which Seurat perhaps intended to convey the sonorous sound of the instrument. Everything in the painting is considered, studied and painted without emotion and thanks to this the scene has acquired a certain unreality. There is something mechanical about it and it is as if Seurat has just stopped all the wheels of this puppet-show. There is little depth in the picture. At the most an illusion of depth is created by the contrast in colour between the double-bass player in the foreground and, for example, the music he is playing from, the stage and the white skirts of the girl dancers. The flatness in the play of lines can be linked with the decorations of Art Nouveau, in which reality is stylized and subordinated to a deliberate mode of design. *Le Chahut* is not a direct representation of reality, but a sample card of Seurat's ideas about art. What he has painted here is not a *café-chantant,* but the mood, gaiety.

THEO VAN RIJSSELBERGHE
(1862–1926, Belgium)

Family in an orchard
canvas, 115.5 × 163.5 cm, 1890

Van Rijsselberghe began this painting in the summer of 1889 before his marriage to Marie Bonnom, which took place at the end of that summer. It is probably the preparations for the wedding that we see being made here in the summery orchard beside the abbey of Aulne at Thuin (Southern Belgium), where the Bonnom family were living at that time. It was in that year, too, that Van Rijsselberghe began

to apply Divisionism in his work, the technique of Seurat and Signac, whom he had met for the first time in 1886. In 1887 Seurat exhibited his famous painting *A Sunday afternoon at La Grande Jatte* in Brussels with *Les Vingt,* of which Van Rijsselberghe had been one of the founders and in which he played an active role.

In this painting Van Rijsselberghe has used Divisionism in a free way of his own. He is more concerned with the representation of the summer atmosphere and the beautiful light than with the formal, scientifically based analysis of Seurat. The picture still has something impressionistic

about it, but on the other hand, the figures are lucidly grouped. The two women in the foreground (the one on the right is the wife of Henry van de Velde) are placed on the two diagonals and lead the spectator into the painting. The central figure sits on a line that runs through the painting from top to bottom. Further back the fourth woman is walking towards the right, while the fifth, behind the tree, is seated facing left. There is no contact whatsoever between the women, each of whom is absorbed in what she herself is doing, and that strengthens the atmosphere of peace and quiet on this summer afternoon.

PAUL SIGNAC
(1863–1935, France)

Breakfast
canvas, 89 × 115 cm, 1886–87

Signac's meeting with Seurat in 1884 determined his further development. From that moment on he, too, set himself to study colour and the effects of colour contrasts in accordance with the spectrum. This painting is one of his early Divisionist works, in which he came close to Seurat. Both artists painted subjects that are also to be found in the work of the Impressionists: landscapes,

the sea, interiors, this painting having a parallel in, for example, *The meal* (1879) by Monet, for whom Signac had a great admiration. In these comparable themes the radically different approach of Divisionism comes out very clearly. In *Breakfast* Signac has used mainly blue and yellow, orange and green as contrasting and complementary colours. The figures (his mother and grandfather and the servant girl) are shown frontally or in profile, standing or sitting motionless and devoid of any expression of feeling. They are not portrayed as individuals but rather as types, as representatives

of a timeless bourgeoisie. In that sense the painting is also a critical commentary on the self-sufficiency of bourgeois life, of the authoritarian capitalism that Signac and his friends turned against. They were anarchists, who tried to further human progress on the basis of personal individual study. They admired Kropotkin and there is a parallel to be found between the method of work of the Divisionists and his idea that social progress ought to come from the possibilities offered by modern technology.

JOHANNES THORN PRIKKER
(1868–1932, Netherlands, Germany)

Madonna in tulip-land
canvas, 146 × 86 cm, 1892

One of the things that characterizes the painting of around 1900 is a new vision of the use and significance of line, colour and form as the means of conveying the essence of things, of human feelings and behaviour.

Here Thorn Prikker has painted the Madonna at the foot of the Cross in the typically Dutch landscape of a bulbfield. The subject is a religious one, but Thorn Prikker wrote of it to a friend in 1894: 'Yet I don't give the Christ or Madonna of the Bible – I regard them simply as pure things. In my work a head of Christ is not meant to be anything more than *something pure,* like a person who is pure or a flower or a day or night... This is just conveying the essence of things, the essence is the mystical existence of things. You see, a flower is a flower with petals and a centre, but a flower is undoubtedly something more than that as well'. In this painting the use of line is all-important and by means of it Thorn Prikker has also expressed the emotional values he connects with the subject. He himself wrote of lines of restlessness, power or saintliness. We can detect an echo of Seurat's ideas here and there is also a vague reminiscence of the stipple technique of the Pointillists. But Thorn Prikker uses all these means in a decorative way of his own. The colour is in a sombre range of grey-green tones and calls to mind an enamelled surface. It is not surprising that Thorn Prikker was to turn later on in Germany to the applied arts, mural painting and stained glass windows.

JAN TOOROP
(1858–1928, Java, Netherlands)

The sea
canvas, 46 × 50.5 cm, 1899

From 1883 to 1885 Toorop studies at the Brussels Academy, making many contacts at that time with Belgian painters and writers from the circle of *Les Vingt*. In 1885 he himself became a member of this group of artists, which organized international exhibitions of modern art in Brussels. There, at an early stage, he got to know the work of Van Gogh, Gauguin, Cézanne, Redon, Seurat, Signac, Van de Velde, and innumerable others. Seurat showed his large painting *La Grande Jatte* in Brussels in 1887 and his ideas and painting technique had a great influence in Belgium and Holland. Toorop made use of Pointillism from 1887 to 1891, after which his symbolistic (see elsewhere) work became strongly linear. A second Pointillist period began around 1898 and it was in those years that he painted this little picture. Notwithstanding the stipple technique, *The sea* is linear thanks to the horizontal bands of the breakers and the bands of colour on the beach, and as a result the whole composition has become decorative. Before beginning to paint Toorop drew the composition on the canvas and he then tried to render the atmosphere and light exactly with colour. To this extent one can call this picture impressionistic rather than divisionist in the manner of Seurat. Through Toorop various other Dutch artists took up Pointillism, including Bremmer. Around 1900 the avant-garde exhibited with *Les Vingt* and the importance of this group is reflected in the collection of the Kröller-Müller Museum. Mrs. Kröller bought work by nearly all the artists who exhibited with *Les Vingt*.

WILLIAM DEGOUVE DE NUNQUES
(1867–1935, Belgium)

The blind house
canvas, 63 × 43 cm, 1892

This painting dates from the years when Degouve imbued his pictures with a mysterious emotional value, which cannot be more closely defined and by reason of which he is numbered among the Symbolists. What is unusual in his paintings is that he pictures the magical by means of subjects taken from reality and in this sense he foreshadows the work of Magritte and what has been called the magical realism of an artist like Willink.

With an almost naïve accuracy he has here painted a pink house between living and dead trees (in what season of the year?), which is vaguely illuminated in the green night from some invisible source. From the upper windows light shines out of the empty rooms, while behind the lower ones the curtains are closely drawn. In the background stands a second house hidden in the darkness, but with one lit window. The sky is full of stars. Everything is quite still, but full of tension. *The blind house* (also called *La maison du mystère*) could be the title of a story and Degouve may have been inspired here by Edgar Allan Poe, whom he greatly admired. He himself was on terms of friendship with many writers, including Maeterlinck and Verhaeren. Through Jan Toorop, with whom he lived in the same house in Machelen in 1884, and Henri de Groux, he exhibited in Brussels with *Les Vingt,* in which all the forces and new ideas of that time came together. The climate of Belgian Symbolism held a great appeal for Mrs. Kröller and she bought 17 paintings and several pastels by Degouve de Nunques.

CHARLEY TOOROP
(1891–1955, Netherlands)

Still life
canvas, 60 × 45 cm, 1935

A still life with rope, a bottle, a mug, bread, ears of corn and a knife – a stiff, dour painting and one that, by the look of it, was created with difficulty. The representation is realistic yet stylized: the contours are sharp, the play of light and shadow is strongly accentuated, the colours are direct. Charley Toorop painted the picture in 1935, when Willink (among others) was preoccupied with a quite different, detailed and menacing realism, that is also termed 'magical realism'. This still life is not in the least magical. It compels the spectator to look at it in quite a different way. It is intense and honest and the objects have 'become symbolic without being abstract. They are not "signs" but images which answer to reality and have a fundamental significance in life' (Hammacher). That fundamental significance is bound up on the one hand with the life of Charley Toorop herself (one might see a similarity here to Van Gogh, whom she greatly admired, in the sense that her work is a reflection of her life) and on the other with the political and social situation between the two world wars, to which Charley Toorop reacted with Communist leanings. As the daughter of Jan Toorop she had grown up in a sheltered, artistic and devoutly Catholic environment, in which she had had to fight her way to an independence of her own, a struggle that in her view had points in common with the hard life of the people of Westkapelle on Walcheren where this still life was done. The tension between hard reality and the going beyond that reality (the metaphysical) is implicit in it.

PABLO PICASSO
(1881–1973, Spain, France)

The Madrileña
panel, 52 × 33 cm, c.1901

The young Picasso was completely open to
all the artistic expressions he saw, whether
from the past or of his own time, but it was
the expressive and symbolistic currents in
particular that attracted him: Van Gogh,
Munch, Toulouse Lautrec, the Pre-
Raphaelites, Beardsley, Steinlen, Toorop,
Daumier. He was interested on the one
hand in the decadence of the Fin de Siècle
and on the other in the artists of anarchist
tendencies, who took the lot of the
oppressed to heart, his melancholy work of
the Blue Period stemming primarily from
the latter.

   In 1901 he spent a short period in Madrid,
where he made illustrations for the satirical
anarchist paper *Arte Joven*. This portrait of
the Madrileña was probably also done at
that time – it is painted in an exaggerated
Pointillism, a method of work Picasso used
in a number of pictures around 1901,
including one of a dwarfish woman,
inspired by the dwarf in Velasquez' *Las
Meninas,* and another of a defiant, greying
prostitute from the streets of Madrid. The
hardness of those two paintings is, however, absent from the portrait. The dreamy
face is framed by the bright orange hair,
the white dress and the blue-green background, while the hat, in tones of blue,
white and yellow, rounds the composition
off at the top. Although the range of
colours is borrowed from the Impressionists, Picasso uses it in a full, expressive
manner, comparable with that in the work
of Van Gogh, for whom he had a great
admiration at this period.

PABLO PICASSO
(1881–1973, Spain, France)

Standing nude
gouache, 62 × 46 cm, 1908

Colour and form, two essential ingredients of a painting, were each re-examined at the end of the 19th century and new possibilities were discovered for both of them. With the Impressionists the accent fell on colour and this was carried to extremes of brightness by Van Gogh and *Les Fauves* (the wild beasts). In Seurat colour and form achieved a harmony, while Cézanne let form be created out of colour. The quest for new starting-points entailed a search for new sources from which inspiration might be drawn and the fact that Gauguin had recourse to a culture outside Europe may perhaps have had an influence on the reappraisal of African art, which was so important to Picasso and others. Picasso saw new formal possibilities in African masks and wooden sculptures and under their influence, as well as those of Cézanne's ideas about basic forms (cone, sphere, cylinder) and Seurat's principles of systemization, he arrived at Cubism, in which he freed form and space from reality. In this drawing of a female nude it strikes one at once that the colour is limited to a greyish-brown tone. The forms of the body are reduced to simple volumes, deliberately distorted and bearing no relation to reality, while the head has clear traces of a Negro mask. This is the first stage of Cubism, in which the forms are subjected to extreme simplification in order to be analysed thereafter.

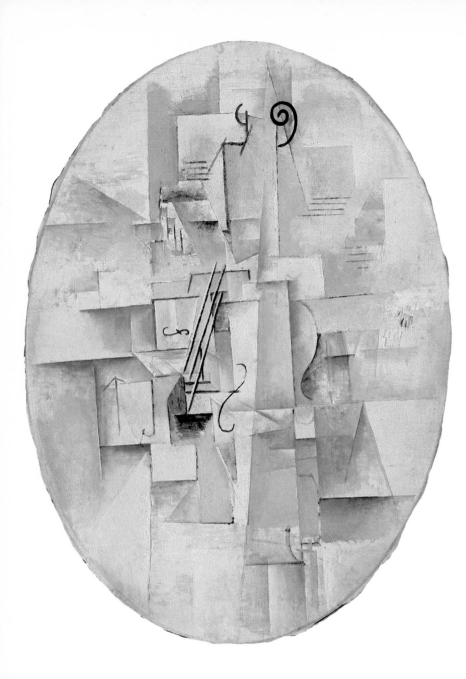

PABLO PICASSO
(1881–1973, Spain, France)

The violin

canvas, 100 × 73 cm, c.1912

This painting is an obvious example of what is known as 'analytical' Cubism. Here too the colour is kept to greys and brown ochreish tints. The arrangement of the forms and planes, on the other hand, is extremely complicated. The objects the Cubists started from were analysed and taken apart with a complete abandonment of illusionistic perspective, so that all sides could be seen at the same time. Everything is exposed, including that which we cannot in reality see: 'I wonder whether we ought not to paint things as we know them, rather than as we see them' (Picasso). Through this unfolding, this flattening out of the object an almost two-dimensional structure is created, a network of planes lying beside and behind one another, and the object thus analysed then passes over into a background that has been taken apart in the same way. If no limits were imposed on it this network could continue to run out on all sides. Here the limitation is indicated by the oval and it may be noted how the whole painting is built up from the centre (where the most concentrated forms are to be found) and runs out towards the frame in ever vaguer forms.

In Picasso and Braque the analysis often goes so far that the starting-point, a given object from reality, can no longer be recognized. Because of this, signs are added to the painting which are meant to make the theme clear, as here the treble and bass clefs, the curve of the body of the violin and the shape of the sound holes. The space element is still clearly present here in the planes which can be seen from the shadows to be lying one behind the other.

JUAN GRIS
(1887–1927, Spain, France)

Still life with oil lamp
canvas, 48 × 33 cm, 1912

In 1906 Juan Gris (a pseudonym for José Gonzalez) went from Madrid to Paris, where he joined up with the group of painters which included Picasso in the Bateau Lavoir. At that time he made illustrations for various periodicals (*Le Charivari, Le Cri de Paris,* etc.). By 1910 he was making naturalistic drawings, but it was not until 1911 that he did his first Cubist work. His first pictures of this time were characterized by a great clarity in the forms, which were painted in a simple grey-blue colour, sometimes accentuated by scattered planes in light blue, yellow, ochre and a pinkish grey.

Gris' Cubism is quite different in character from that of Picasso and Braque. In his view their complicated networks of small planes, in which the object could scarcely be discerned any longer, were too arbitrary and unclear. His approach to Cubism was less emotional. He was the intellectual who set to work in a methodical way. In his first still lifes there is obvious influence from Cézanne in the broken contours and the geometric forms. There is a balance between the abstract and reality and all the forms, whether of the objects or of the background, are linked together. In this picture there may perhaps also be some influence from Seurat, *i.e.* in the directions of the movement (vertical and two diagonals, but not horizontal), which look like beams of light. This painting is abstract in essence, but it gives the suggestion of a still life.

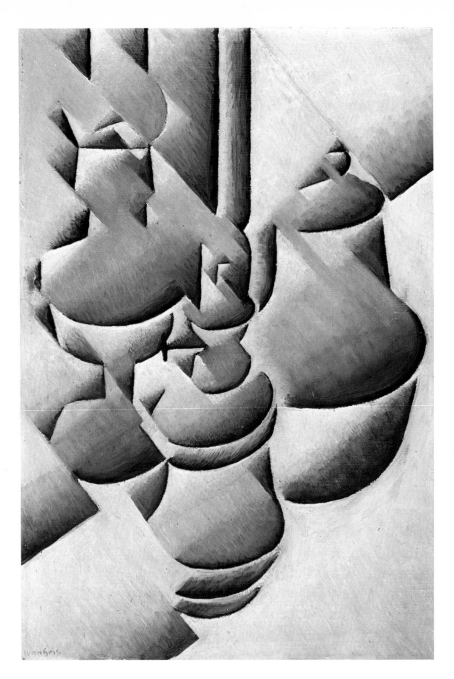

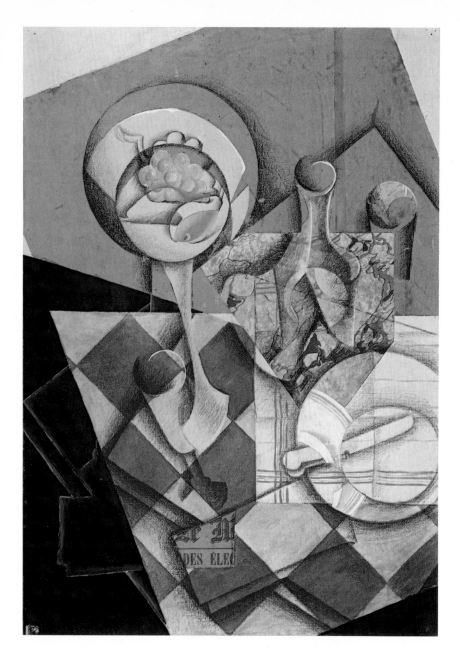

JUAN GRIS
(1887–1927, Spain, France)

Collage with fruit dish and carafe
black and blue chalk and oils on paper and
canvas, 92 × 65 cm, 1914

Gris used collage in his work for the first
time in 1912, when he painted a picture of a
washstand and stuck a real piece of mirror
glass on to the canvas to represent the
mirror. On another painting he pasted a real
label on to a bottle in abstract form. Picasso
and Braque also used this technique around
1912 to make their unrecognizable abstract
objects recognizable again. In Gris' work it
was also connected with the ambiguity
within a painting, emphasizing the relationship between reality and what was painted.
On one of his collages he pasted a piece
from a newspaper, on which was printed *le
vrai et le faux* (the real and the unreal), thus
indicating this dualism still more clearly.
For the Cubists collage was a means of
achieving a synthesis between abstraction
and reality, it being possible to work out a
composition more or less unconnected
with reality and yet to suggest reality
nonetheless. The French rejected complete
abstraction such as was being developed at
this period by, for example, Kandinsky.

This collage by Gris evinces a great com-
plexity. Most of the canvas is pasted over
with pieces of paper and the pencil lines
show that the first drew the composition
on the canvas and then stuck on to it pieces
of paper cut to shape (on which he first
drew and painted). In these (real) pieces of
paper we see suggestions of a newspaper, a
marble table, a floor with black and white
tiles, a tablecloth. With highly geometric
forms Gris has made a composition in
which real and unreal are fused into an
independent whole. It is a synthesis of abstraction and reality that runs parallel to the
unity of spirit and matter that Mrs. Kröller
regarded as the ultimate goal of art and life.

JUAN GRIS
(1887–1927, Spain, France)

Still life with carafe and lemon
panel, 55 × 38.5 cm, 1916

In this strongly composed still life Gris has used wood as a background, the grain of it forming an essential expressive element for the entire painting. The regular vertical structure of the wood is interrupted again and again by the things painted on it, but it remains a unifying factor. In addition Gris has, by using it, achieved great transparency, since we can see the background not only through the glass of the carafe and the goblet, but equally through the newspaper, the surface of the table and the lemon. As a result the objects are dematerialized, all of them thrusting through one another. But a balance is again provided for this transparency in the form of the dark silhouettes, which Gris uses over and over again in a great deal of his work and which give the impression of a strong light falling on the objects. Thus there are three superimposed layers: the background, the silhouettes and the objects. The colour is determined by the wood, against which Gris has used black, brownish-red, yellow, white and grey-blue, very carefully weighed colours which buttress the composition. It may be difficult to see this clearly on the reproduction, but Gris has framed the whole composition with a narrow white border, which is probably meant to keep the vertical movement of the wood within bounds. The museum possesses a number of drawings by Gris of similar still lifes, which clearly show how intensively he worked on these complicated compositions.

FERNAND LÉGER
(1881–1955, France)

Three nudes in a wood
canvas, 120 × 170 cm, 1909–10

This sombre, enigmatic painting could be called an act of homage to Cézanne, for whom Léger had a deep admiration. Cézanne had said that there are three basic forms in nature, the cone, the sphere and the cylinder and it was on this statement that Léger based this painting, in which he simplified everything to those geometric forms. Moreover, the subject is also derived from the numerous *Bathers* painted by Cézanne. Three nude figures can be made out: one standing on the left with arms upraised, another slightly lower down seated facing left and a third standing on the right with one arm upraised. Léger wrote about this picture: 'I wanted to carry the painting through in volumes as far as possible... It has been said that there are influences from the Douanier in this canvas [Rousseau le Douanier, who painted exotic landscapes in his spare time]. That is true, perhaps, since I saw his work at that time, but it is subconscious... I regarded the *Nudes in the wood* simply as a battle of volumes. I thought that I ought not to introduce any colour into it, for I already had enough with the volumes'.

Léger was a Cubist, but he followed a different path from Picasso and Braque, arriving also at quite different solutions, in which volume as a plastic element is central. He was continually looking for contrasts, in forms, colours and subject-matter, and in that sense he spoke the language of a new era, of the twentieth century which is so rich in contrasts.

FERNAND LÉGER
(1881–1955, France)

The typographer
canvas, 54 × 46 cm, 1919

Léger stated in 1914 that contemporary
painting ought to be representative of the
new visual environment that had come
into being through the evolution of the
new means of production. He eulogized a
new beauty, that of the machine. He saw
and felt that the machine, *élements mécani-
ques,* was coming more and more to dominate daily life. In the machine he saw 'the
human gesture which has been standard-
ized and given form in structures that
function'. At that time people saw in technology, in a more naïve way than now,
a guarantee of a better future, a prospect of
a new quality of life and it was in this that,
around 1920, Léger found the subjects with
which he bore witness to his own time. His
attitude towards this new beauty was different, more subtle and positive, than that
of the Futurists, who went to extremes in
their adoration of the machine and its
destructive power.

The painting *Three nudes in a wood*
already has something mechanical about it
in a certain sense, but it is also restless,
almost chaotic in the piling up of the
volumes. This painting of 1919 is much
quieter and the composition is carefully
weighed. The subject, the typographer,
comes from a world that has to do with art
as well as the machine. What Léger has
painted here is not a human being, but a
machine, surrounded by planes and forms
in bright colours; everything points to the
mechanical, even the stencilled letters that
indicate uniformity and the possibility of
reproduction. One could perhaps also say
that the picture points to democracy, to
equal opportunity for everyone, a thought
Léger was always preoccupied with,
especially later on.

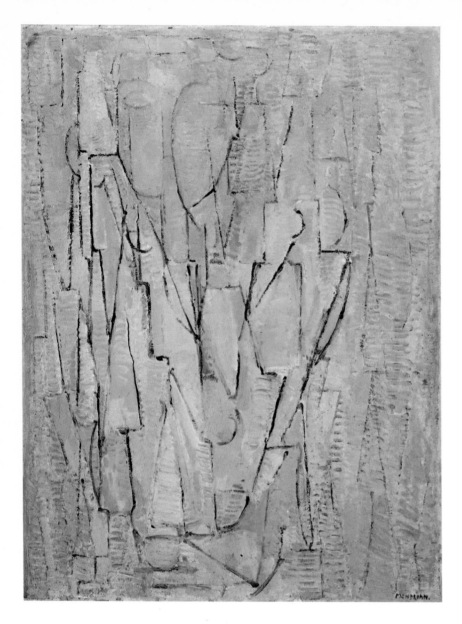

PIET MONDRIAAN
(1872–1944, Netherlands, France, U.S.A.)

Composition XI
canvas, 76 × 57.5 cm, 1912

In 1912 Mondriaan went to Paris. Through the work of Cézanne, Picasso, Braque and others, which had been on view in 1911 at the first exhibition of the *Moderne kunst-kring* (Modern Art Society) in Amsterdam, and through his contacts with Dutch artists living in Paris (Kickert and Schelfhout), he had come into contact with Cubism. It attracted him, because he saw in it a spiritualization of form, which offered new possibilities for his own development. His earliest work had been naturalistic and from there, under the influence of Toorop, Van Gogh and Seurat, he had arrived at a stylization of forms and above all of colour, with which he tried to represent his emotional experiences with regard to reality.

This painting clearly shows the influence of the analytical Cubism of Picasso, in which forms are taken from reality and set down in a complex structure (see Picasso, p.90). Mondriaan has used the same brown-grey colour range as in, for example, Picasso's *Violin,* and he has taken as his starting-point for this painting a portrait of a woman, which he has taken apart in planes of different forms derived from the triangle, the rectangle and the circle. Apart from the eyes there is nothing in the painting that still reminds us of the portrait and as with the Cubists, so here, the composition is built up from the centre outwards, the edges remaining open.

In Paris Mondriaan began to free himself from reality and in this he was to go further than the Cubists. 'Through not wanting to say or relate anything human, through the complete negation of oneself, precisely that work of art appears that is a monument of Beauty, above everything human and yet precisely human in its depth and universality'.

PIET MONDRIAAN
(1872–1944, Netherlands, France, U.S.A.)

Composition in line and colour
canvas, 88 × 115 cm, 1913

Starting from analytical Cubism Mondriaan achieved a clarification of his form. The planes, which in *Composition XI* were still fairly arbitrary and painted almost expressively, have in this painting become rectangular and more rigid in line. Mondriaan also abandoned the brown-grey colour, going back again to the pink, green, blue-grey, ochre and violet that he had used in Zeeland in 1909. The only thing that is retained here is the increasing vagueness of the lines

towards the edges of the canvas. This painting no longer has a subject from reality as its starting-point, although it is certainly reminiscent of architecture, an effect brought about by the use of mainly horizontal and vertical lines, varied here and there by segments of circles.

Around 1910 Mondriaan wrote to a friend: 'For me it is a truth that by not wanting to say *anything definite* one says precisely what is most definite, the truth (which is widely all-embracing). For me the greatest art is without doubt the architecture of the Ancients. I think it is possible by horizontal and vertical lines, constructed *deliberately,* but not *calculatedly,* and guided

by high intuition and brought into harmony and rhythm – I think that with these basic forms of beauty – if necessary augmented by lines in other directions, or curved lines if need be, one can arrive at a work of art that is as strong as it is true'. That interplay of the horizontal and the vertical was to determine his later work, which was simplified in colour to the primaries and in form to relationships. If there is still a painterly element discernible here, later on, around 1920, the paint was applied to the canvas stiffly and impersonally so that nothing should detract from the idea of universal beauty.

PIET MONDRIAAN
(1872–1944, Netherlands, France, U.S.A.)

Composition No. 10 (Pier and Ocean)
canvas, 85 × 108 cm, 1915

In 1914 Mondriaan made what was meant to be a brief return visit to the Netherlands, but was compelled by the onset of the war to remain there until 1919. During those years the *De Stijl* group was set up with Mondriaan as one of the signatories of its manifesto (1918). He spent a lot of time in Domburg, where he made what are known as his plus-minus compositions. He again drew inspiration for his work from themes from reality: the church at Domburg and, as in this painting, a pier extending out to

sea and flanked by piles. There is no colour in this composition, about which Mondriaan wrote to Bremmer, who was supporting him at this time and also buying work by him for Mrs. Kröller: 'It had been my intention to do it in colour, but I had no more time and I found that it did nonetheless express what had to be expressed'. In 1916 he deliberately made a composition in black and white and that was also bought by Mrs. Kröller.

Composition No. 10 differs from the other paintings discussed here in that lines are used for their own sakes and no longer form rectangular areas. A mobile structure has been created out of little vertical and horizontal lines, sometimes crossing each

other, sometimes not. It can be said that there are no forms and no colours in this painting.

Mondriaan wrote at this time: 'The positive and the negative by themselves disturb the unity. They are the source of all misery. Agreement between positive and negative means happiness'. Positive and negative signify horizontal and vertical, by which Mondriaan expressed male and female, matter and spirit, the real and the unreal. His thesis of the positive and the negative tallies with Mrs. Kröller's idea of the unity of spirit and matter, but in his later work, in her view, there was too little of matter (reality).

PIET MONDRIAAN
(1873–1944, Netherlands, France, U.S.A.)

Composition in diamond form
canvas, 49 × 49 cm, 1919

Mondriaan made four compositions in diamond form between 1918 and 1920, a period
in which he was concerned with achieving
greater clarity in his work, an abstraction
that would stand entirely on its own. The
diamond frees the painting from its traditional form and makes it an independent
object. In addition, the bounds imposed by
the frame no longer bear any relation to
what is taking place on the canvas, which
means that attention can be focused more
strongly on the painting itself. At this
period Mondriaan was using grids, horizontal and vertical lines within which he
could apply a clear arrangement. In the
rectangular paintings of this grid period the
frame works in with the arrangement on
the canvas and also indicates the boundary
of that arrangement. These two solutions
show how concerned Mondriaan was with
finding his own way to what he termed
Neoplasticism. He eventually opted for the
rectangular enclosure for his work,
although he did make one or two more
diamond-shaped paintings later on (around
1933).

In this composition the lines are painted
in a grey tone and the colours are already
moving towards primary red, blue and
yellow, while the white is still greyish. The
grid on the basis of which Mondriaan
determined his arrangement is still vaguely
visible in the background and here and
there he has introduced improvements.
This painting marks the beginning of his
later work. 'The spirit constructs most
purely by means of the simplest line and
making use of only the most primitive
colour'. The longer he went on the more
Mondriaan was to work from the spirit, the
intellect and intuition, rather than the emotions, which to him were too personal and
not universal enough.

BART VAN DER LECK
(1876–1958, Netherlands)

The fruit-seller
canvas, 79 × 46 cm, 1913

Van der Leck began as a glazier in the glass workshops in Utrecht where the stained glass windows were made for the numerous new Catholic churches that were built in the Netherlands at the end of the last century. Only after that did he go to the National Academy of Art and the National School of Applied Art in Amsterdam, working as an independent artist from 1904 onwards. Starting from the monumental art of Derkinderen and the symbolistic style of Jan Toorop he arrived around 1910, via various intermediate stages (including a Breitner-like Impressionism), at a stylized manner of his own, which he was to develop ever further in the direction of abstraction (see p.101).

In this painting, *The fruit-seller,* this stylization is clearly present and we can see in it, too, how Egyptian art was a source of inspiration for Van der Leck. The faces and figures are seen either frontally or in profile, while the faces have no personal features, but are virtually uniform. The colours are bright and although they have not yet become primary, they are nonetheless already greatly simplified. The subject stems from Van der Leck's work of around 1906 in Amsterdam, when he began painting street scenes and working-class figures. Another aspect is the composition: the scene is set entirely in the plane of the canvas, while the way in which the figures and the stall follow the frame of the painting shows that Van der Leck was accustomed to working for an architectural setting. Throughout his life he was preoccupied with the relationship between painting and architecture, which is one of the essential foundations on which his work is based.

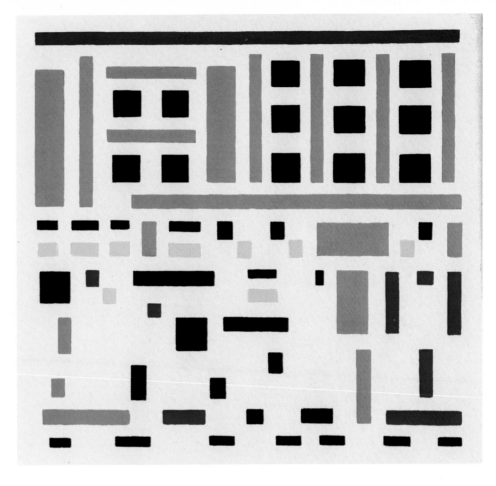

BART VAN DER LECK
(1876–1958, Netherlands)

Composition 1917, No. 4
canvas, 94 × 100 cm, 1917

During the years 1916 to 1918 Van der Leck worked in an abstract manner, making paintings in which small blocks in the primary colours – red, blue and yellow – and black are set against a white background. These abstracts, which he called 'mathematical images', are the last stage in a stylization of reality that had continually been carried further and further. All the abstract paintings of this period are based on themes taken from reality, in each case themes he had already painted earlier.

This *Composition No. 4* is derived from *Leaving the factory,* a painting he had made in 1910. The process of carrying the simplification ever further can be followed from the surviving drawings and gouaches he made for this painting, but although it is interesting for its own sake, it is not the process that is important, but the end product, the way in which he has arranged the formal elements on the picture plane and determined the sizes and colours of the blocks. He made two versions of all the paintings he did in 1917, one with an open structure, the other with a heavier effect, as here.

An essential characteristic of these paintings is the separation of the formal elements on the picture plane, there being no links between them. Through this the painting regains a spatial element that had been lost during the process of simplification. It was precisely in this that Van der Leck saw the possibilities for painting in conjunction with architecture: painting introduces space by means of colour and 'makes the walls open', as opposed to architecture which encloses space.

VINCENT VAN GOGH
(1853–90, Netherlands, France)

Woman gleaning
black chalk, light wash, 525 × 435 mm,
summer 1885

It is remarkable how important the time in which Van Gogh worked in Nuenen was for his later life in France and especially for the years in Arles, St. Rémy and Auvers. In Arles he described *The potato eaters* as the best thing he had done up to then. In this he was not so much concerned with the technical qualities of his work, but rather, and much more, with the intention behind it. And that intention meant reproducing the essential, the more than reality. As we have already seen, he always spoke of Millet as his model: '...from Millet one can best learn to see, perhaps, and acquire "a faith"'. It was a faith in peasant folk, in the hard-working people of whom he himself was one. In their life he saw a parallel with his own. 'To give the *peasant figure in action,* that's what a figure is – I say it again – essentially modern – the heart of modern art itself. Ostensibly there is nothing simpler than painting peasants or rag-pickers or other workers, but – no other motifs in painting are as difficult as those everyday figures'.

His style of drawing in his Nuenen period gave complete expression to his intention. These are very powerful drawings, in which light and dark play a big role. The figures are drawn in dark, heavy forms in keeping with their exacting work, with not the slightest striving for refinement or detail. This drawing of a woman gleaning is a splendid example of this.

VINCENT VAN GOGH
(1853–90, Netherlands, France)

View from Van Gogh's room at St. Rémy
black chalk, pen and brown ink,
475 × 560 mm, autumn 1889

This is one of the many drawings Van
Gogh made of the view from his room in
St. Rémy. Working in the confinement of
this room, he put his moods and also his
memories into his numerous paintings and
drawings of this theme. Sometimes there
are reapers at work in the cornfield,
labouring peasants whom he had so often

drawn at Nuenen. He writes of how the
corn is flattened after a thunderstorm and
how the sun rises over the field or how he
has wanted to imbue it with an atmosphere
of calm and great peace. Occasionally he
shows it raining there and this drawing
seems to herald or perhaps record the end
of a shower of rain. It was done first in
black chalk and then further worked up
with the reed pen. The enclosed cornfield
has a peacefully waving motion, but behind
the wall the landscape is more chaotic,
more full of 'a striving for a piling up of
things; one will do this by a way of

drawing that tries to express the confusion
of the masses'. This duality is repeated in
the sky in the calm, radiant sun over against
the turbulent cloud. The mood is threaten-
ing on the one hand and peaceful and
positive on the other. This contrast seems
to tally with Van Gogh's own situation: in
October he wrote, 'The weather is lovely
out of doors, yet, I don't know why, I
haven't been outside my room for a long
while, not for two months. I would need
courage to do that'. The contrast lies in the
peace of his cell as against the threat of the
outside world.

JAN TOOROP
(1858–1928, Java, Netherlands)

Le retour sur soi-même
pencil with, in our opinion, ink and water-colour, 165 × 180 mm, 1893

As we have seen, Toorop worked in the Pointillist technique up to 1891. After that his work became more linear and the content of his drawings and paintings Symbolist in character. Here, too, he was stimulated by his contact with *Les Vingt* and the Symbolist literature of his day. In his own Symbolist work his subject-matter is simple in principle: the struggle between the earthly, the sensual, death and temptations on the one hand and the good, the heavenly and the innocent on the other. The atmosphere in which this struggle is carried on is highly mystical, line being for him the form best suited to the representation of this mysticism, this spiritualization. He was half Javanese by birth and this comes out in his Symbolist work in the figures which are often like *wayang* puppets.

This drawing is oriental and Buddhist in its content: the withdrawal into oneself, the introspection, whereby one dismisses the world outside oneself (note the upraised hand). On the back of it is written *Le miroir d'une vie,* which may refer to Toorop's own life. He sought for a better life (which in his case meant mysticism) and in the end he found it, through examining his own soul, in the Catholic church.

The female figure in this drawing is as it were a prototype of the good. She also crops up in many of Toorop's other Symbolist drawings: the maiden bearing a candle who shares in that better life that is 'serene and continually perfecting itself'.

ODILON REDON
(1840–1916, France)

L'homme primitif
pastel, 560 × 420 mm, c.1915–16

Redon is said to have made this drawing at
the end of his life, but that is an art-
historical comment that needs scarcely be
of any importance in the evaluation of it
and it is even questionable whether it
serves good purpose to say much about it at
all. The source Redon drew on for his
work has already been indicated in the
notes on the two other reproductions of his
work in this book. It was the world of the
imagination, the fancy, which he called his
'guardian angel', the voice of the subconscious which revealed surprising perspec-
tives to him. Anyone who sees his work
can apply his own associations to it or he
can remain open to the suggestions Redon
puts to him. That this drawing raises questions is evident from the fact that it has
been given three different titles: *Man,
Primitive man* and *The hunter*. All three
point to the suggestion that the silhouette
of the walking figure could be the prototype of the first man, of primeval man, 'on
his way towards light, but unknown
distances, on his way to *sonores clartés*'
(Redon), to clear insight. One can readily
imagine that such a striving and longing
was present in someone who throughout
his life and certainly at the end of it placed
the visible at the service of the invisible.

HENRY VAN DE VELDE
(1863–1957, Belgium, Germany,
Netherlands, Switzerland)

Woman at the piano
pastel, 230 × 290 mm, 1892

From the dedication written on this
drawing it appears that Henry van de Velde
gave it to *De Haagse Kunstkring* (the Hague
Art Society) in 1892, when he gave a lecture
to the Society on 'The Peasant in Art'. The
request to give a lecture will probably have
come from Toorop or Thorn Prikker, who
knew Van de Velde from the exhibitions
of *Les Vingt* in Brussels. He may perhaps
have chosen the subject under the
influence of Millet and Van Gogh, two
painters whom he greatly admired at that
time for their obstinacy and individual
rebellion. He himself was full of doubts at
that period about his existence as a painter
and much occupied with the problems of
the day, with how to bring art to the whole
community, with anarchism and Marxism.
His admiration for Van Gogh also comes
out in this drawing. It was mainly the work
from St. Rémy that he had seen in Brussels
in 1890 and from which he took over the
sinuous, emotional play of line, after
having previously worked in a strict
Divisionism. In 1894 he saw all the work
Van Gogh had left at the home of Theo
van Gogh's widow and that moment was
for him the decisive one at which he gave
up painting to devote himself to the decorative arts and architecture. This drawing
comes from the collection of the Leuring
family, for whom Van de Velde built a
house in Scheveningen in 1903.

GIACOMO BALLA
(1871–1958, Italy)

The flight of the swallows
tempera on cardboard, 490 × 695 mm, 1913

In 1909 the Italian poet Marinetti published an article in the Paris newspaper *Le Figaro,* in which, for the first time, he set out the ideas of Futurism, a movement he himself had called into being. It was a manifesto the purport of which tallied with that of later Italian Fascism. Marinetti glorified danger, aggressiveness, the machine, speed, war, militarism, patriotism and the future, calling for the destruction of everything from the past, the museums and the libraries; art must now be steeped in violence and crime.

Futurism found its way into literature, music, art, the theatre and politics. In painting and sculpture (see also p. 118) it was characterized by a less aggressive depiction of movement, of the dynamic. Balla was one of the Futurist painters (he often signed his work *Futur Balla*), who from 1912 on concerned themselves with the lines of force of movement. This study of flying swallows, with indications in the background of a door, electricity wires and the angular line of a roof gutter, was further worked up by him in a painting that he called *Moving lines and dynamic sequences.* We can see many successive movements, which are extended into the static parts (*e.g.* the door and the gutter), and there is an effect that can be compared with the succession of separate images in film, which was so modern at that time.

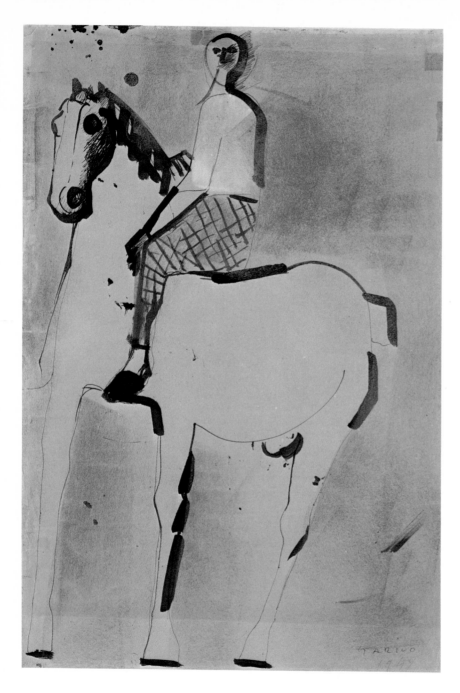

MARINO MARINI
(1901–80, Italy)

Rider
pastel and ink, 465 × 320 mm, 1949

The theme of horse and rider has been a constantly recurring one in Marini's work since 1936. For this there are, of course, points of contact in plenty to be found in the immediate surroundings of someone who has spent all his life in Northern Italy (albeit as far as Marini is concerned Etruscan and T'ang art are perhaps even more important than the equestrian statues in Padua, Venice and Ferrara). However, when a theme is so continuously present in an artist's work, there must be a more personal and emotional reason behind it. This clearly emerges also from the very different relationships between horse and rider that appear in these series. In this drawing the rider is sitting quite straight and relaxed, but sometimes he is flinging up his arms in panic and the horse seems about to rear and throw him. In several sculptures the horse is standing on its hind legs and the rider has disappeared. The artist must have experienced all these different phases of unity, disturbed equilibrium and powerlessness in the relationship between man and animal with great intensity for this theme to have held its own in his work for so many years, with such expressive power and without ever giving the impression of routine or dull repetition.

A fascinating aspect of Marini's drawings of 1940–50 is the rhythm of the heavy black accents that crops up in them over and over again. The accents seem to have been gouged out of the drawings and as a result the forms are held together in a more concentrated way.

WESSEL COUZIJN
(1912–84, Netherlands)

Seated man

pen, 278 × 215 mm, 1950

This drawing has all the qualities of a sculptor's drawing without being a direct study for a piece of sculpture. Through the arrangement of the arms and the drawn-up right leg the whole body has – almost – been reduced to the form of a block and the monumental way in which the arms, legs, coat and head are rendered shows so strong an emphasis on volume that it is patently clear that a sculptor has been at work here. The axis from the head to the left knee and the heavy 'beam' of the arms determine the structure, while the left leg is so powerfully positioned that it almost takes on the function of a post on which the sculptural block rests.

Later Couzijn did his drawings in a different style. After having for years devoted himself primarily to sculpture, he 'suddenly' came up with a majestic series of drawings after a visit to Mexico in 1973. In them he evokes images in a veil of sensitive, whirling pencil lines.

He has always occupied a place all his own among the artists of his time and there is no trace to be found in his work of influence from modish currents. The war years, which he himself spent in America, inflicted an inner wound on him and his sculptures are often imbued with a feeling of being submerged, a feeling of powerlessness. His search for an interplay between different materials and his bringing together of different sculptural objects in such works as *Table and bed, Auschwitz* and *Science fiction* reflect his attentiveness to the way in which people and things influence each other.

ALBERTO GIACOMETTI
(1901–66, Switzerland, France)

Large figures in the studio
pencil, 450 × 300 mm, 1958

Between 1947 and 1960 Giacometti made
series of elongated, attenuated figures on
great club-feet. Sometimes, in his drawings,
these figures stand askew in steeply sloping
surroundings. He seems to have started out
from a vision of man being eaten away by
forces in space, while also trying to
discover the minimum material presence
with which man can still hold his own in
space. The figures are pierced by the architecture of the interior and the contours of
people and things are suggested rather than
indicated by the multitude of lines, this
suggestion losing certainty by the feet in
particular.

In 1960 Giacometti had a long development behind him, in which the surrealistic
element had been very marked right from
the beginning. But it is a surrealism that is
worked in in a completely unique way,
because the connection between the particular experience of space and the particular
terrors in space is so strong.

The figures in his drawings stand or sit,
often facing forward or else reduced to
total insignificance, in a large space, or else
they are entirely enclosed in a cage of lines.
In this drawing it is quite clear that what is
primary is not the faces, the hands or the
feet, but the attitudes – the stiffening. If
Giacometti draws the eyes in a face this
adds the intensity with which the figure is
gazing at the artist, *i.e.* the artist is gazing at
and absorbing his model.

CONSTANT
(b.1920, Netherlands)

Great labyrinth
pencil and black chalk, 1412 × 1287 mm, 1966

Constant once said, 'Drawing is such a
natural process, it's like writing letters. It's
your handwriting' (see Fanny Kelk on
Constant, Amsterdam, 1974). Although he is
best known for his paintings and construction in perspex, as well as his essays for,
among other things, *Nieuw-Babylon,* he has
always continued to draw, no matter what
else he has been doing.

This drawing is connected with his *New
Babylon* studies, New Babylon being the
name he coined in 1959 for 'the city of the
future', which he had already been occupied with for years, both in his thoughts
and in maquettes. It was envisaged as an
a-functional, playful city, which it would
only be possible to build after the social
revolution, a city that would call on the
creativity that he regarded as being innate
in everyone.

A city in transparent stages at various
levels linked by ladders or flights of steps
and in various colours. The visual
adventure is very important: again and
again a different area is created that
demands a different orientation. It is
characteristic of Constant that he does not
adopt a purely poetic approach to the architecture, but constructs it entirely in
accordance with 'normal' technical data.
This drawing shows a completely firm
structure and extremely solid forms, but
some of his other drawings, including
examples of the same year, are much more
playful and full of improvisation.

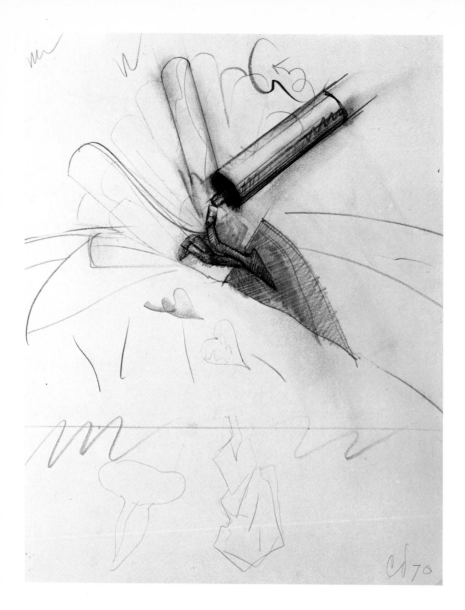

CLAES OLDENBURG
(b.1929, Sweden, U.S.A.)

Study for a trowel
water-colour, 354 × 280 mm, 1969–70

Oldenburg is a born draughtsman and a born maker of notes. He always carries notebooks with him, in which he jots down the thoughts and images that come to him, and he collects these notes in files in loose-leaf form, around 600 sheets a year. For a long while he hesitated as to whether he would become a writer, a painter or a 'sculptor', but actually the choice never needed to be made, since it is perfectly obvious that he is all three all the time. And even when he uses water-colour or chalk or a pen, he handles them in a highly painterly manner.

At no period in his life has his work been abstract. His sketches (and his sculptures too) always concern things from his daily life, whether at home or in the street. For a time (around 1961) it was possible to posit an affinity with Dubuffet in his interest in the chaotic, amorphous, confusing and sur- prising impressions to be discovered on a walk through the city, but all the same Dubuffet is, broadly speaking, more con- cerned with the people and Oldenburg with the things in the street. The affinity with Pop Art, too, is highly relative. Olden- burg shares the same wish (or choice) to limit himself to everyday, possibly vulgar reality. But in his case there is an underlying contemplativeness that goes further and deeper than in the others, because his wonder.is directed not only at things, but also and more particularly at the use that is made of them, including the use he himself makes of them in his work (*i.e.* as an artist).

RICHARD SERRA
(b. 1939, U.S.A.)

Untitled
charcoal and black chalk, 1265 × 960 mm,
1972

All Serra's sculptural projects are accompanied by drawings. They are not preliminary studies or records of the final results, but Serra tries out his ideas on paper as well while thinking out and working on the projects. The steel plates that meet the boundaries of an area (as in the dell in the sculpture park) and that alter the totality of that area become here, on paper, a diamond-shaped plane, the outlines of which are accentuated by the charcoal. The shifting of the outlines clearly demonstrates how the final alignment is chosen from a series of possibilities. Moreover, in this drawing, precisely because of the plurality of the outlines and the presence of the bands of charcoal, the suggestion is created that it has to do with a diamond-shaped body rather than just a two-dimensional plane. It also clearly reveals that what is essential is the process of creation, not the product at which it finally comes to a stop.

This aspect is very fundamental for Serra: he works with molten lead, film and television – all media that militate against coagulation and fixation. The scale and size of his projects also contribute to this. For example, the sculpture he has made near the Stedelijk Museum in Amsterdam is so large that it can only be taken in from a distance and by walking slowly round and through it: the final image of the sculpture is formed by the spectator in the act of walking.

OTTERLO MASTABA (PROJECT FOR RIJKSMUSEUM KRÖLLER-MÜLLER) 283,000 STACKED OIL DRUMS (EACH 50 lt.) h. 25,3 m × 63,2 × 52,4 H.

CHRISTO
(b.1935, Bulgaria, U.S.A.)

Mastaba project, Otterlo
chalk, 1270 × 915 mm, 1973

In 1973 there were plans, or perhaps we should say dreams, in being for making a monument over 25 metres high in an open place in the wood near the museum out of 283,000 oil drums. The monument has not yet been realized, but Christo did make a series of drawings to show the effect that would be created in the wood where it was to have been built.

In 1966 in particular he had been engaged on piles of oil drums of various colours and in connection with each project he made a series of drawings, often in enamel paint on cardboard. The most extended work consisted of 1,240 drums for an exhibition at the Institute of Contemporary Art in Philadelphia. He had already, in 1962, closed off the Rue Visconti in Paris near Pierre Restany's Galerie J with a wall of oil drums. The marks Esso, Total, Shell and BP were clearly visible, Christo wanting to show by this that he was merely using the drums in another situation and that it was not his intention to achieve a shift in their function (e.g. by making them into 'aesthetic objects'). He was concerned at that time only with achieving an extension of functions by using the drums as barricades or, in Otterlo, as a pyramid marking a situation. All the same his piles of drums inevitably acquire aesthetic undertones in museum surroundings, since in relation to museum objects attention is focused on form, colour, texture and other aesthetic qualities.

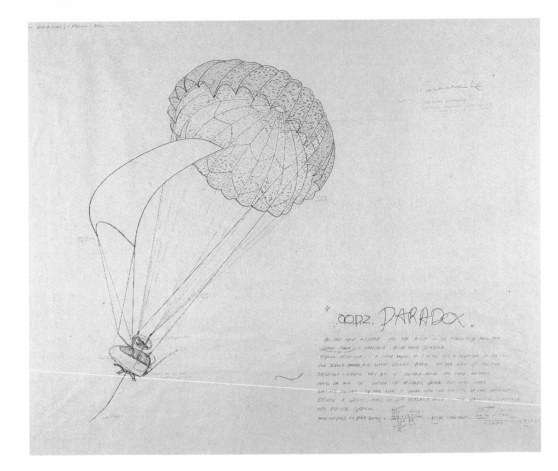

PANAMARENKO
(b.1930, Belgium)

OOPZ Paradox
*1st motor propeller parachute to slow
down the air* ± *7 metres or more*

pencil and coloured pencil, 95 × 150 cm,
1975

Panamarenko created a furore in Antwerp in the sixties by organizing happenings and publishing the paper *Happening News*. His appearances were accompanied by glamour and uproar: dressed as an airline pilot or in an all-white suit, he introduced himself as a 'multimillionaire'. His passport gave his profession as balloonist. From 1966 onwards his work had a process-like character. It was exhibited in Anny de Decker's White Wide Space Gallery. He used plastics for preference, but did not stop short at displaying his own snowed-under boots as well. There is a relationship here with *Arte Povera,* which was then spreading through Europe. Around 1968 Panamarenko began to develop the mechanisms that were to lead to the prodigious collection of castles in the air that he dreamed up. In splendid drawings he designed aeroplanes with propellers driven by manpower. The age-old idea of the flying man, which Leonardo da Vinci still thought it possible to realize, exists in Panamarenko's work in another form. His winged vehicles are not the realization of a dream, but the proof of its existence as an 'unrealizable' desire. The drawings look like serious designs, provided with an explanation and description of the technical components, the whole giving the impression of being related to modern science. On one occasion Panamarenko tried to make his gas-filled *Airship* (a Zeppelin-like monster) become airborne. To his great relief, he did not get a metre off the ground.

Africa, Bambara (Sudan)

Upper part of a mask
wood, h. 59 cm

Around the turn of the century many artists became very interested in African tribal art. They no longer regarded these figures and masks as ethnographical curiosities, but saw them as artistic expressions of a world unknown to them. While it was primarily the unfamiliar, primitive forms that had a direct influence on their work, the magical character of this sculpture played a role as well. Picasso, Matisse and Derain in France and Kirchner and Schmidt-Rottluff in Germany were among those who were already incorporating the African forms into their own art at an early stage.

This upper part of a mask comes from the Koutiala area in western Sudan, where the Bambara tribe lived. They worshipped Chi wara, a mythical being in the form of an antelope, who they believed had created the first Bambara and taught him to till the land. In all the ceremonies that had anything to do with fertility – seedtime, harvest, initiation rites for boys and girls – the Bambara performed the Chi wara dance, using masks of male and female antelopes, which always appeared in pairs. All the Chi wara masks have the two horns and the mane in zig-zag form, sometimes highly stylized in character, sometimes very naturalistic.

This antelope mask was acquired for the Kröller-Müller Museum in 1955. In this a gap can be said to have been filled, for along with a seated figure of a man from the Baule tribe the mask represents the great diversity in that African art that was of such importance to the Cubists, whose work is so strongly represented in the collection.

Mexico, Colima

Standing figure
basalt, h.47 cm, between 500 and 900 A.D.

From his voyage of discovery Columbus brought back to Europe art treasures from Mexico, but they were objects sheathed in gold, not stone statues. Albrecht Dürer admired them in Brussels in 1520 with the words: 'I have also seen the things brought for the King from the New Land of Gold: a sun entirely of gold... and all manner of wonderful things meant for every sort of use'. Real interest in the art of Pre-Columbian Mexico did not arise until 1928 when the exhibition *Arts Anciens d' Amérique* was held in Paris. For many artists this meant the discovery of a new formal world, which had surprisingly good affiliations with, in particular, those sculptors like Henry Moore and Wotruba who were expressing themselves in pure, stylized forms.

The sculptures of Pre-Columbian Mexico show an abstraction of reality that points to the world of the myths that dominated the whole life of the country at that time. Everything was at the service of the gods, *i.e.* of the forces of nature which were given form by the sculptors, who were also priests. In those forms they depicted the inhuman, horrible, and unapproachable aspects of metaphysical forces that cannot be understood by man. The sculptures were purposely made non-naturalistic, being geometrical, cubical and stylized in form to symbolize the time-lessness, the greatness and the power of these gods. The statues are mostly kept within the closed mass of the stone, details being incised in the stone or carved on the surface. In this sculpture, which is thought to represent Huehueteotl, the god of fire, these characteristics can clearly be seen, while the face has the form of a menacing mask.

UMBERTO BOCCIONI
(1882–1916, Italy)

Forme uniche della continuità nello spazio
bronze, 117 × 39.5 cm, 1913

Boccioni was primarily a painter (and draughtsman). He only made ten sculptures, but they are very important, since they give a lucid summing-up of the formal principles that were propounded by the Futurists. That he was concerned with giving expression to principles, which had come to him through his observation of people and things, is also clear from the title of this sculpture, *Unique forms of continuity in space*. What has struck him here is not so much the moving man as the changes in form that occur when he sees a figure moving in space, and especially the fact that the forms change continually when the movement goes on in space without a break. In the case of the Cubists there is a singular movement: the observer (the artist) moves round the object and gives expression to all the facets of the thing he is walking round. In the case of the Futurists the movement is a plural one: not only does the observer (the artist) move, but the figure does so as well, rushing past with giant strides (or, in other cases, a cyclist coming along on his racing bicycle, a crowd of people pouring on to the street in rebellion, etc.). When Boccioni models the head of a woman, he realizes how much the model and its surroundings form a single, moving entity, not only because it seems as if the forms are continually changing as a result of the changing light, but also because little vibrations and changes can continually be observed in the model itself.

Boccioni also perceived in the work of Medardo Rosso an intensity of the same sort as that with which he himself observed and depicted these phenomena. After years of neglect the value of Rosso's work was recognized – for what was in fact the first time – by Boccioni and his friends.

JEAN TINGUELY
(b.1925, Switzerland, France)

EOS IX

iron, 260 × 250 cm, 1966–71

Around 1955 many artists became fascinated by technology, either cursing it or making use of it through such things as electric motors or projectors. Right from the start (c.1945) Tinguely adopted an approach entirely of his own: his preoccupation with machinery (there is always a moving element in his sculptures, mostly worked by electric motors) has a strongly playful aspect. But he says, *'Ich spiele wütend'*. His fury is directed against everything that is slick, cerebral, systematic and humourless: his machines rattle, creak, grind and squeak, their movements are jerky, illogical and abrupt. Thus he presents a different, an absurd use of the machine. Sometimes, too, he destroys the sculpture, or rather, he lets it destroy itself. Working in collaboration with his wife Niki de Saint Phalle and his friend Luginbühl, he makes ever bigger machines, of which the parts are more massive and the noise often deafening and menacing. But the fury never blots out the playfulness: humour and irony always break through the aggression. And in this he marks himself off from many Dadaists of the twenties. He is heart and soul a carnival reveller and his feeling for, or rather faith in, the value of the old folk customs and symbols, which still survive so strongly in Switzerland, has never left him, in spite of his move to France in 1953, and is ever-present in his work.

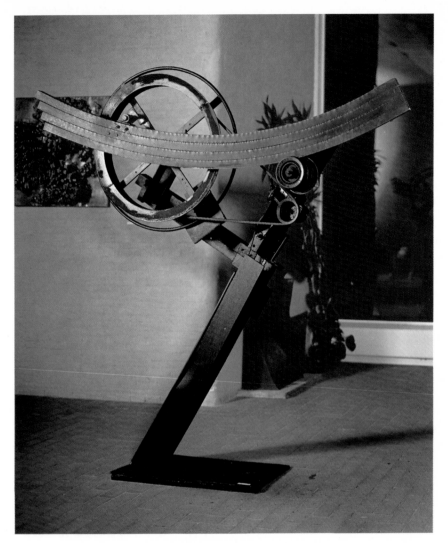

CHAIM JACOB LIPCHITZ
(1891–1973, Russia, France, U.S.A., Israel)

Sailor with guitar
plaster, 76.2 × 30 cm, 1914

Lipchitz worked in Paris, with a few breaks, from 1909 until he emigrated to New York in 1941. In 1912–14 he had contacts with painters like Diego Rivera, Juan Gris and Picasso, who at that time were searching for a way of representing form that would be more geometrical and constructivist than that of the previous generation.

    Sailor with guitar evinces a first attempt at this tightening up. The circle of the beret finds a parallel in the abstracted, curved volume of the shoulders and arms, while the left leg, placed forward in a somewhat mannered, not to say precious, way (Lipchitz had seen a sailor dancing like this with a guitar in Spain), forms the left side of the triangle that is continued in the diagonal of the guitar. In the years that followed Lipchitz carried the tightening-up process still further. He came nearest to complete abstraction in 1916 with a series of standing figures, but their very titles already indicate that, though there has certainly been a process of abstraction, they are not purely abstract works. Cubism made it possible for him, through discussions with his friends and working on a long series of standing figures, to overcome the mannerism of his earlier years and to achieve a very strong, highly plastic form, from which all details were omitted, and which was preeminently suited to giving expression in a disciplined way to all the tensions that were in him. The paintings and gouaches he made in those years also show how close the link was with his group of friends: his work is more forceful, that of Gris more objective, that of Picasso more lively and that of Braque more melancholy, but all of it is bound up together. They inspired and supported each other in their creative development and perhaps held each other back sometimes too. Not until 1920, after the First World War, did each of them go his own way, separate from the others, and in Lipchitz himself the involvement with Cubism continued until about 1925.

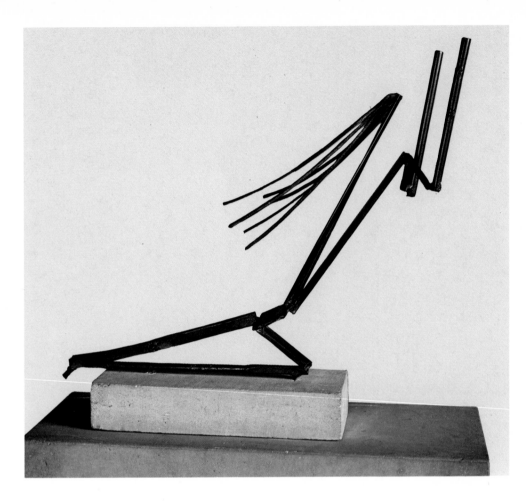

JULIO GONZALEZ
(1876–1942, Spain, France)

Prayer
iron, 76 × 95 cm, 1932

It sometimes seems to be suggested that
Gonzalez made a complete changeover in
1929, that up to then he had always made
drawings, paintings and jewelry and that
afterwards he concentrated entirely and
exclusively on sculpture. But in fact there
also exist sculptures by him of 1910, 1914 and
1927. Thus, while there were certainly
intermissions, the wish to make sculpture as
well was evidently already present much

earlier on. It is, however, true that there is a
difference between the work before 1929
and that made thereafter. Gonzalez' contact
with Picasso in that year, which was very
stimulating for both of them, led them
both to the discovery of the qualities of
iron. This was not such a big step for
Gonzalez, for he had grown up in a family
of goldsmiths and had thus long been used
to handling tongs and welding equipment,
but for Picasso it was different. He was
captivated primarily by the assemblage
possibilities or iron, finding an uncommon
fascination in handling scrap and bits that
had been thrown away.

In *Prayer* Gonzalez has used simple bars
and rods of iron. As always in his work, the
relationships with the human figure are
clearly discernible. It is notable that the
gesture of praying shows no movement inwards, but rather a striving upwards as in
the Greek orantes. With sculptures like this,
in which the expressivity is created by a
highly concentrated, almost calligraphic
gesture in space – an arabesque realized
with an extreme sobriety of means –
Gonzalez exercised a great influence on all
the artists who worked in iron after 1945.

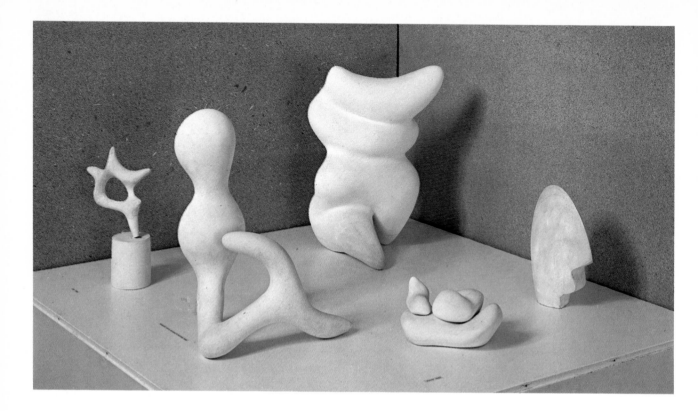

HANS ARP
(1887–1966, France, Switzerland)

Five small Sculptures: Sculpture à être perdue dans la forêt, Torse pré-adamite, Étoile, la Sirène, Tête heaume I

plaster, 11 × 22 × 15.5 cm, 1932; 48 × 31 × 28 cm, 1938; 21 × 17 × 3.5 cm, 1939; 45 × 38 × 24 cm, 1942; 26.5 × 17.5 × 9 cm, 1959

In 1971 Marguerite Arp-Hagenbach gave the museum five little plaster sculptures which offer a very limpid reflection of Arp's method of work. The earliest piece, of 1932, stems from a period in which Arp repeatedly placed small, almost fluid forms on a 'bed' of bronze (*i.e.* plaster) which serves to support them. In the *Étoile* the opening and the minimal supporting point on the base are of great significance. The swelling forms of the *Sirène* and the taut, closed forms of the *Torse pré-adamite* and the *Tête heaume* all belong to a period in which Arp's work came into being 'in parallel to nature', that is, his sculptures show the same pattern of expanding and contracting forms, or, in other words, of forms determined by an inner force, an inner logic, as that which can be perceived in plants.

The idea that the artist does not imitate or reproduce nature, but creates from principles that are related to the formal principles discernible in the plant and animal world, is a very old one. Some artists may arrive at plant-like or animal forms of this sort entirely intuitively, others may study such structures theoretically as well. In Arp's case the process is primarily intuitive, flowing from a mystical feeling of being linked to nature.

MEDARDO ROSSO
(1858–1928, Italy, France)

Child in the sun
wax on plaster, h.34.5 cm, 1892

In a country where sculpture was still based on the Classical and Classicist traditions Rosso took a unique position of his own right from the start. In one of the earliest known sculptures by him *(Embrace under a street Lamp, 1882)* he was already using a method of modelling that is more 'impressionistic' than that of the majority of his contemporaries. Struck by the mobility of light and shadow and the fact that the figures of the man and woman were virtually impossible to distinguish from one another in the half-dark (the light of a gas-lamp is, after all, pretty dim), he was already seeking in this early work for a form in which the articulation of the parts would be subordinated to the form as a whole.

In the nineties, when he lived for a long while in Paris (1889–97), he often worked in wax, for wax is so soft and malleable that even a light touch is enough to produce an undulation and a difference in the play of light on the surface. And it was precisely in the portrayal of little children, who have not as yet developed any pronounced facial features, that he found a possibility of expressing this lack of articulation and the fusion of parts with great consistency. When his sculptures have to be installed in a situation where the light is too bright, it is often difficult to distinguish where the face begins and where the transition is between, for example, an arm and a trunk. For his contemporaries it was very difficult to see this technique as a positive quality, for they, after all, were used precisely to striving for a clear articulation of parts, but it may be that Rosso was strengthened in his completely different approach by the contacts he had with Dalou and Rodin during his time in Paris.

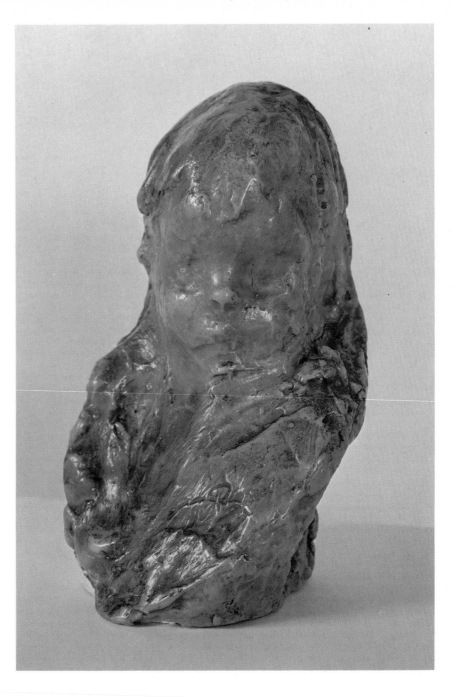

KATARZYNA KOBRO
(1898–1951, Russia, Poland)

Spatial composition 4
painted steel, 40 × 64 × 40 cm, 1929/1979

During her studies Kobro got to know the revolutionary *avant-garde* in Moscow (Tatlin, Rodchenko, etc.). In 1920 she went to Smolensk, where she married the Pole Strzeminski. In 1920–21 she was a member of the Suprematist group Unovis in Vitebsk, along with Malevich and Lissitzky. She lived in Poland from 1924 onwards and also adopted Polish nationality. She belonged in succession to the following *avant-garde* groups: Blok (to 1926), Praesens (to 1926) and 'a.r'. (from 1930). In 1932 she, like Strzeminski, became a member of the international Abstraction-Création group. Virtually all her work was destroyed by the Nazis during the Second World War.

In the formal sense her first sculptures were related to Tatlin's work in their contrasting of different surfaces. After that she explored the geometrical arrangement of planes, reducing her use of colour and developing her ideas towards a functionalist method. To Kobro art (and above all sculpture) was not an escapist means of coming to terms with an objectionable reality. On the contrary, she regarded the artist as a planner and architect, involved in a new ordering of society. The artist supplied scientific models in which colour and plane made the dynamic character of space visible in the most economical manner. The curved planes give Kobro's own sculptures a restrained lyrical feeling.

Spatial composition 4 was given by the Sztuki Museum, Lodz, Poland. This is a unique copy of the original of 1929, which is to be found in the Sztuki.

CHARLES BIEDERMAN
(b. 1906, U.S.A.)

Structurist relief
aluminium, 97.5 × 66.5 × 22.5 cm, 1957–68

In 1937, the year in which in England Ben Nicholson and others were working on the collection of essays entitled *Circle,* Charles Biederman was in Paris, where he had contacts with the members of *Abstraction-Création.* The misleading term 'abstract', which Naum Gabo had wanted to do away with, since every work of art (even a figurative one) is both an abstraction from reality and a concrete thing, had made its debut.

Biederman incorporated his European impressions and his own conclusions into his masterly book *Art as the evolution of visual knowledge,* which was written between 1938 and 1946, but not published until 1948. In his artistic work he confined himself entirely to the making of reliefs, mostly in very brilliant colours on hard material (aluminium), whereby the colours were made to radiate out very powerfully into the area around them and the things in that area were reflected in the relief.

Biederman's writings had a great influence on artists in Europe; and in England and the Netherlands in particular there arose a second generation of Constructivists (or Constructionists), who were supported in their quest by his ideas even more than by the ideals of the Russian Constructivists and *De Stijl.* The predominance of the relief, especially among the English artists, is probably also bound up with his studies: it is a development of the possibilities of 'colour in architecture', whereby the artist and the architect keep their independence.

125

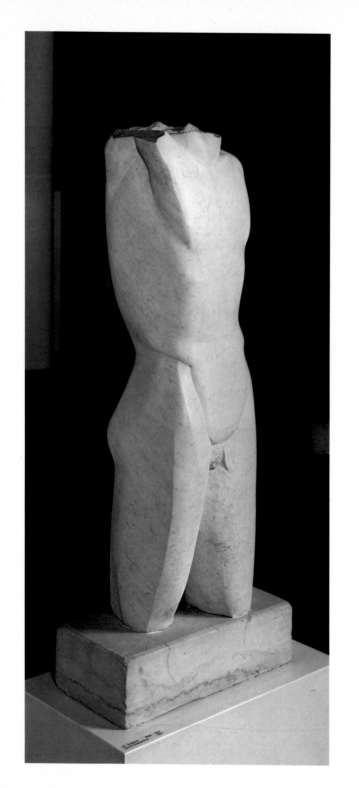

OSSIP ZADKINE
(1890–1967, Russia, France)
Torso: Clementius
marble, h.98 cm, 1941

Zadkine, who emigrated from his native
country to settle in France in 1909 after a
three-year transitional period in London,
always made use of a variety of materials as
means of expression: plaster, wood, stone,
marble, terracotta. His forms were strongly
influenced by the material he was using
and what might seem at first sight to be
inexplicable – the contrast between the
simple, rigid forms of most of the wood
and stone sculptures and the tormented,
baroque forms of many of the bronzes –
can largely be put down to his great feeling
for the qualities of the material.

This marble torso was made in the years
when Zadkine lived in New York: like
many other artists he fled from France to
the United States in August 1941 during the
German occupation. *Clementius* must have
been one of the first sculptures he made
then. He used a pillar from a monumental
sculpture of a negro (Clementius), working
the remains of the original Victorian decoration into the neck as an indication of hair.
He made use on more than one occasion of
a calligraphic element in his work, drawing
a profile, a hand, a sprig of flowers or hair
in thin, incised lines. Here again there
would seem to be no conflict between two
different methods of work, but rather a
great sensitivity towards the various possibilities discovered while handling the
material.

DAME BARBARA HEPWORTH
(1903–75, England)

Pastorale
Serravezza marble, 65 × 110 cm, 1953

In 1939, when the threat of war became too great, Barbara Hepworth moved with her family from London to Cornwall. This move, which was made for external reasons, had a radical influence on the development of her work. In her youth she had experienced the landscape of Yorkshire with great awareness; now the landscape of Cornwall became, for 36 years, the inexhaustible source of inspiration for her work. That is not to say that the forms of shells, stones or hills can be detected literally in her work, but all her perceptions, all her thoughts and her whole life were so strongly centred on the landscape around her that there came into being almost a symbiosis between herself, her work and all the forms and phenomena of nature.

From this contact with nature, too, she derived in those difficult war years and later her faith in the indestructibility of positive forces. By experiencing herself as a reclining, standing, sitting or moving figure in nature she came to realize, as she herself said, that 'there is no landscape without the human figure: it is impossible for me to contemplate pre-history in the abstract. Without the relationship of man and his land the mental image becomes a nightmare. A sculpture might, and sculptures do, reside in emptiness; but nothing happens until the living human encounters the image' (Barbara Hepworth, *Carvings and drawings,* London, 1952).

The completely relaxed feeling of a person lying down, who knows the sea and the hills (the crests of the waves and the troughs) around him, found expression in this *Pastorale.*

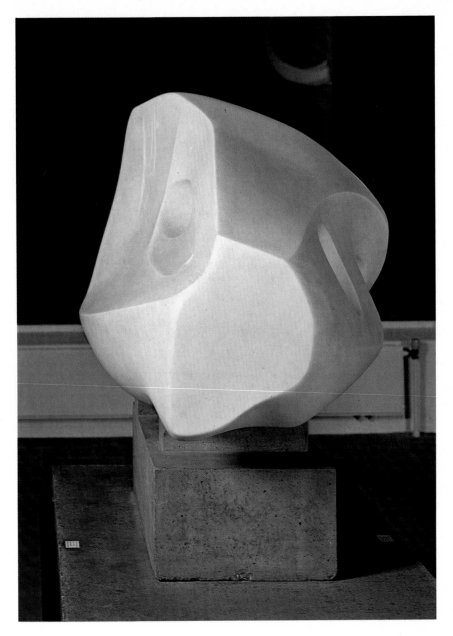

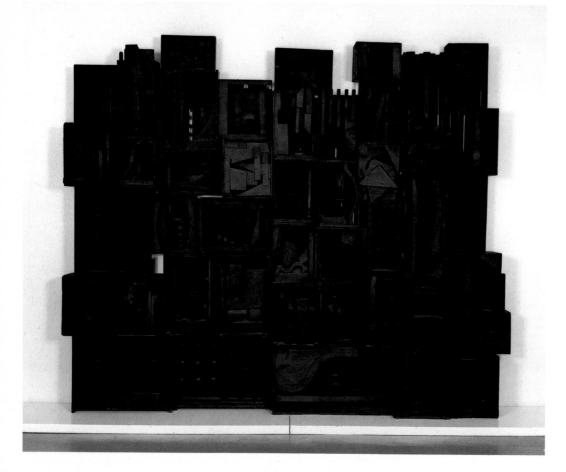

LOUISE NEVELSON
(b.1900, Russia, U.S.A.)

Sky cathedral III
wood, painted black (45 chests),
300 × 345 cm, 1959

A piling up of little chests filled with odd bits of wood that have been found here and there, often on rubbish dumps. Sometimes the chests are nailed up and completely closed. For the artist, however, this piling up has a completely different meaning: they are not bits of wood, but magic objects in an edifice that has acquired an effect entirely its own through the way it is divided up and through the dimensions of the chests. This sacred character is further strengthened by the colour: black or white or gold. Nevelson only made large scale works like this between 1959 and 1968, but the need to build an environment, a stage, is something she has always felt: as happens in the theatre, she recreates the reality of everyday life and constructs a new dramatic reality around her. Thus a single piece, such as may be seen in a museum or private collection, does not in fact fit in with her intentions. For her it is a process starting from a single given form that continually goes further and further: the 'sculpture' can become ever larger or smaller, higher or lower. She presses on along all the walls and over all the rooms in her house. The material can change: for a while, for example, she worked in metal or perspex and the forms then became more strict and geometrical and lost their *objet-trouvé* character, but the method and the vision remain the same.

The penetrating, almost magical effect that comes out of the sculptures, also radiates from Nevelson herself. Heavily involved in all discussions about the social position of artists, and especially women artists, in her country, she exerts a unique fascination on her contemporaries in spite of her advanced age (and partly because of her great erudition).

CARL ANDRE
(b.1935, U.S.A.)

Henge on Threshold (Meditation on the year 1960)
wood, 5 elements, each 30 × 30 × 150 cm,
210 × 150 × 30 cm overall, 1971

A henge is the magic circle in which rituals take place. It is surrounded by a bank and ditch, with an inner enclosure of wood or stone. When Andre stayed in the South of England for a time in 1954, he experienced Stonehenge as a sculptural setting. The work *Henge on Threshold* seems to be a reminiscence of this experience in which a part stands for the whole: as an elementary construction it is a reflection of the architecture of Stonehenge, as sculpture a remembrance of a place.

From 1967 onwards Andre became known primarily for his metal floors. These consist of identical elements placed loosely beside each other so that one can walk over them. When one stands on them, it becomes possible to feel the weight and resistance of the metal (*e.g.* of lead, aluminium, zinc, copper, steel, magnesium). These sculptures were laid out by Andre himself and in doing so he always tried to find a relationship with the surroundings. 'Sculpture as place' is for him emphatically material in its significance, open to all.

He is classed as belonging to that movement in art which from 1965 onwards became known as 'Minimal Art'. By comparison with other important representatives such as Judd, Flavin and Morris, Andre is the most classical, thanks to his choice of material. He has a great admiration for the work of Brancusi *(Endless Column),* while the early work of a friend of his youth, Frank Stella (*Black Paintings,* 1958–59; *Aluminium Paintings,* 1959–60), was of equal significance for the sharpness of his formulation.

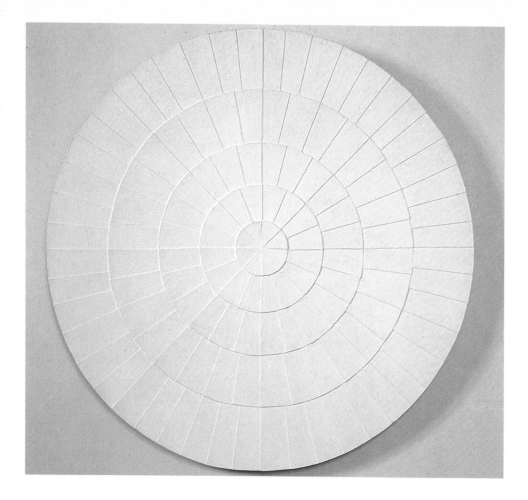

JAN SCHOONHOVEN
(b.1914, Netherlands)

Relief R 71-4
papier-maché, diam. 120 cm, 1971

In 1957 Schoonhoven in company with Armando, Henk Peeters, Jan Henderikse and Kees van Bohemen set up the Dutch Informal Group which later, in 1960, developed (without Van Bohemen) into the Nul Group (parallel to the Zero Group in Germany of Piene, Ücker and Mack). The Informal Group placed the emphasis on the spontaneous movement of the hand, the Nul Group on the reduction of all the possibilities of colour and form to white and the simplest possible formal element which was or could be repeated over the whole surface.

Schoonhoven began making reliefs in papier-maché in 1956. The pattern is determined by the lines of shadow or, as here, light, that form the contours of the pieces of white paper stuck on white. Because everything is cut and stuck by hand, there always remains a minimal irregularity which, when it repeats itself, clearly influences the total image. In addition, the fact that the white shows all sorts of nuances of whitish 'colours' in a changing play of light (not only on the relief itself, but also with equal effect on the wall on which it hangs) gives the relief an extra dimension, so that it never appears pale and remote.

Of recent years Schoonhoven has also made very big reliefs for large wall surfaces. In these he has sometimes had to seek assistance with the cutting and sticking. This has very occasionally resulted in a slight loss of sensitivity, but the principle remains the same and just as authentic.

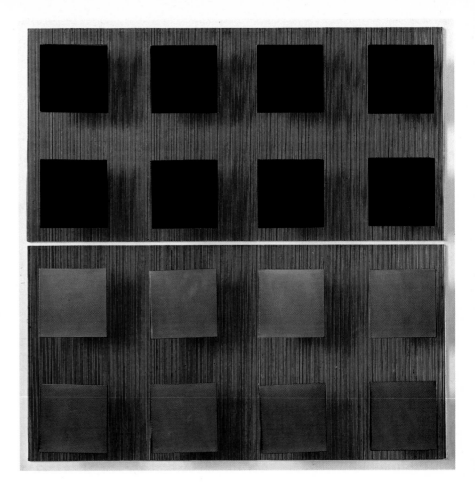

JESUS RAPHAEL SOTO
(b.1923, Venezuela, France)

Relief: relations pures
wood, metal, 105 × 105 cm, 1965

Soto, who settled in Paris in 1950, has been working since 1951 in the field of Kinetic Art. At first the element of movement was achieved by optical illusion, *i.e.* by the movement of the spectator past a relief on which the possibility of optical illusion was created by a close, moiré grid. After 1958 moving or vibrating elements were fixed in front of the panel to which the grid of horizontal or vertical (painted) lines was applied.

Soto is steadily increasing the scale of his work, seeking more and more for cohesion with large architectonic areas and even, on occasions, with nature. Partly as a result of this the participation of the spectator becomes even more intense: now he no longer merely walks past vibrating walls, but he moves about inside Soto's work, which surrounds him on all sides *(les pénétrables)*. Of the artists engaged in Kinetic Art Soto is the one who has achieved the richest development of possibilities with the greatest variety of forms.

The Galerie Denise René in Paris supported these artists from 1944 onwards, being the first firm of dealers to do so. In 1960 the artists joined together to form the *Groupe de Recherche d' Art Visuel.* Soto himself never belonged to it (he had after all been occupied with Kinetic Art long before 1960), but he has always been on friendly terms with its members and has shown his work in company with theirs (see Morellet, p.132). There is, however, a stronger feeling for refinement and aesthetics in his work than in that of his fellow-artists (Copains) and as a result his whole approach and development are apparently less systematic and less disciplined than is the case with the others.

131

FRANÇOIS MORELLET
(b.1926, France)

Sphère-trame
aluminium, diam. 180 cm, 1963–67

In 1960 Morellet was one of the founders of the *Groupe de Recherche d'Art Visuel* (see Soto, page 131). From the beginning he aimed at an interplay of chance and regularity, making use of a grid system in his work. The relationships (in this case the corners) that form the lines of the grid were determined 'by chance', but worked out systematically. Morellet's encounter with the work of Mondriaan in the fifties

had a decisive effect on the development of his own work. Although he makes many prints and also works in oils, colour plays no great role.

The emphasis on the playfully determined system is so strong that the personal element is completely relegated to the background: for the spectator it becomes at least as important to work out the rules of the system as to experience the optical effect. This factor carries with it every possibility of having the work executed by a computer, as well as that of working out variations on the basic theme (the chosen grid) in a series.

Morellet also frequently makes use of light (fluorescent tubes) that goes on and off according to a set programme. Through this the spectator becomes disorientated in time and space and this disorientation, this feeling of instability and relativity, is precisely what these artists are after. This idea also saves them from rigidity: the grid is always different and the way in which it is seen, *i.e.* experienced, is always different as well. It depends on the play of light, the place of the spectator and the speed at which he is moving.

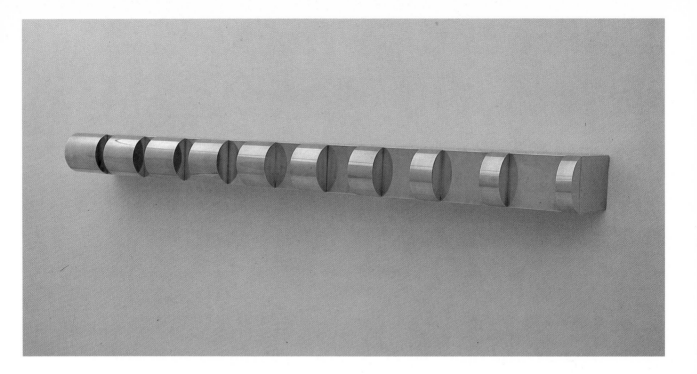

DONALD JUDD
(b.1928, U.S.A.)

Untitled
brass, 12.5 × 21.5 × 175.5 cm, 1969

In 1965 Judd published the article 'Specific Objects' in which he made it plain in no uncertain terms that, as far as he was concerned, the traditional media of painting and sculpture were finished. He opted for 'real objects in real space', for art that is stripped of illusion and that belongs in all senses to three-dimensional reality. This attitude was in part a reaction to the thin Abstract Expressionism of around 1960, a movement which he could no longer relate to what he himself felt.

Judd studied art history and philosophy at Columbia University in New York, passed through various art schools and worked for years as critic for *Art Magazine*. He demonstrated his intentions with his first exhibition in 1963 (Green Gallery, New York): wooden boxes painted cadmium red stood about, unrelated, on the floor. The contours were sharp, the form was lucid and there was not a single allusion to any meaning of any sort.

After this there followed a big series of sculptures made up in accordance with very simple principles of arrangement. The blocks placed beside one another on the floor at regular intervals, the horizontal reliefs ('progressions') and vertical reliefs ('stacks') possess an immediately perceptible clarity. The elements are identical with one another and there is no question of composition (the bringing of dissimilar components into a meaningful relationship). In this brass relief of 1969 the open spaces between the enclosed volumes are just as important as the volumes themselves. The first open form on the left corresponds with the first closed form on the right and so on.

CHRISTO
(b.1935, Bulgaria, France, U.S.A.)

Empaquetage
wood, board, padding, cloth, string,
125 × 181 × 38 cm, 1961

Christo, who lives in New York, became generally known through his spectacular projects *Vallery Curtain* (Colorado, U.S.A., 1972) and *Running Fence* (California, U.S.A., 1976).

The latter was realized only after years of legal battling, but, after initial opposition, virtually the whole of the population of the area through which the screen snaked (total length 24.5 miles) were warmly in favour of it. In the end the work existed for two weeks, making the wind that swept over the bare hills visible in continual movement. At the same time, however, the screen was a barrier, a wall that abruptly shut off the landscape and seemed to divide the world in two. The invisible part had perhaps never been seen by anyone; perhaps it did not even exist at all.

Christo made his first *empaquetages,* among which the example at Otterlo is one of the most intriguing, as early as 1961. He also packed up objects such as perambulators of motorbikes. He arrived in Paris in 1958 after fleeing from Prague. His first works were classed under *Nouveau Réalisme,* but it soon became clear that his intentions went further than a concern for strictly artistic problems.

The enormous scale of his projects would be inconceivable without equally great organizing ability, his wife Jeanne-Claude taking a large share in that side of the work. Numerous projects have so far failed to get any further than the design stage (*e.g.* the packaging of the Reichstag in Berlin and the Pont Neuf in Paris). This also applies to his piles of oil drums (see p.114), the largest of which was proposed to the sheikh of Abu-Dhabi.

MARIO MERZ
(b.1925, Italy)

Praehistoric wind from icy mountains
oil on canvas, neon tube (red), neon numbers, faggots, 201 × 200 × 59 cm, neon tube 312 × 2.5 cm, 1963–78

Merz' art consists of the creation of transitional situations; his sculptures (better described as situations) are created as temporary provisions, as the expression of the nomad who wanders about the world and takes no possession of things, so that the world cannot take possession of him. Literally everything can serve him as material; once it is brought into the situation Merz wants it to be in, it changes into a sign in a process that knows no beginning and end, but exists only in the here and now, as the here and now through which time flows. Merz' art is a dynamic art full of individual poetry, which resides without reservation or intellectualization in the reality from which, according to him, all legends and mythologies (and is not art itself a mythology?) proceed.

In the work *Praehistoric wind* the shaft of light pierces through the shield that only a moment ago seemed a reliable protection against irrationality from outside. In the faggots glows the light of a procreation beginning and expanding on all sides. The numbers 1, 1, 2, 3, 5 constitute the beginning of the Fibonacci series, a series based on the procreation of rabbits, starting from a pair (1 + 1) without the power of nought and represented graphically as a spiral. This system, whereby each successive number is found by adding the two previous numbers together, crops up in much of Merz' work, along with the form of the igloo, the shelter he builds for himself out of the materials he finds: plates of glass and clay, bamboo canes, aluminium tubes, putty, lute, plaster or wax, earth and faggots: all mixed up together and in flat contradiction to each other. Merz binds them loosely together: the permanent chaos assails the classic image because the latter is static and does not look for its meaning in the here and now.

At the end of the sixties Merz was included in *Arte Povera,* a movement which, with Merz, Kounellis, Paolini and Fabro, has outlived Minimal and Conceptual Art.

DAN FLAVIN
(b.1933, U.S.A.)

Quietly to the Memory of Mia Visser
blue fluorescent light, 2640 cm, 1977

The first tube to 'speak for itself' dates from 1963: fastened to a neutral wall at an angle of 45 degrees. With an exhibition in the Green Gallery (New York, 1964) and by dedicating two works to Judd and LeWitt, Flavin placed his light sculpture in a context that was from 1965 onwards to be known as Minimal Art. Titles play an important part: by the mention of the name of a person to whom the work is dedicated after the neutral *Untitled,* that work acquires an individual note and meaning. Sometimes this is private, but it can also relate to a well-known person. The title *The Nominal Three (to William of Ockham)* of 1963 is of particular significance. Ockham (d.1349), an excommunicated Franciscan, made a distinction between faith and knowledge and held that reality consists only of individual things, an important idea to Flavin.

Flavin does not handle light as a universal, spiritual abstraction. He uses fluorescent tubes of different sizes and colours as elements in his work. Light is for him a substance of which the source is measurable, since it tallies with the length of the tube. In his work the shine of the light – the extent and visibility of its range, the essentially intangible radiation on the surroundings and the people moving about within them – has a concrete and particular, as opposed to a universal, origin.

In 1977 he executed a light sculpture inside a pedestrian subway at Cassel, in the context of *Documenta VI.* Plans have already existed for some years for a work in one of the Maastunnels at Rotterdam.

RICHARD LONG
(b.1945, England)

Stone Line
New Jersey blue stones laid on the ground
within a rectangle of 15 × 3 meter, 1976

Since 1967 the subject of Long's work has
been man's relationship to nature, which
presents itself in countless forms as
changing landscape. The term 'Land Art' is
applicable here, since he does not represent
landscape, but lets it coincide with his
material as subject.

From 1966–68 Long studied at the
St. Martin's School of Art in London. In
1967 he walked in a straight line through a
grassy field, until the line had become
visible and could be recorded in a photograph. He always describes his walks as
something that can be measured in time
and distance. He draws the route covered
on a map in a schematic manner (as a
straight line, rectangle or concentric circles)
or he inscribes under a photograph the two
places at which the walk began and ended.
He has a preference for silent, empty
regions like the west coast of Ireland, the
moors of the West of England or the high-
lands of Scotland, but he also journeys
through high mountains like the Andes and
the Himalayas, the deserts of Africa and
Australia and the forests of Canada. During
these walks he makes sculptures with the
stones or branches that he collects in one
spot. The outline is always regular, so that
the presence of a human being is demonstrated in an effective manner, for only the
human intellect is capable of devising a
rectangle or a circle. Long robs nature of its
untrodden inviolateness and he also adds to
it deep human experience.

The *Stone Line* is meant to be laid out
indoors. The natural setting is absent and
has been replaced by a room in a museum.
The stones lie apart from each other as a
field round which one walks. Long's work
is rich in content: in addition to respect for
the romantic tradition that lets critical,
rational man confront nature in doubt and
wonderment, he has, above all, a need to
concentrate this moment within a fixed
compass.

ARISTIDE MAILLOL
(1861–1944, France)

Air
lead, 140 × 255 cm, 1939

This sculpture was not cast until after
Maillol's death, but he himself chose the
material for it. The structure is very clear:
the parallels of arm and legs and the com-
pelling gesture of the hand, which is accentuated by the positions of the head and the
supporting arm, lend the sculpture a severi-
ty that is exceptional in Maillol's work. The
first version of *Air,* which is in stone and
was made in 1939, was placed in the Jardins
Royaux at Toulouse *à la gloire des équipages*

pionniers de la ligne france-amérique du sud.
By reason of a drapery surrounding the
figure and the fact that there is still scarcely
any question of a stylized structure in it, the
Toulouse sculpture fits much more mark-
edly into the context of the serene pasto-
ral figures that are so typical of Maillol than
does the version in the sculpture park at
Otterlo (there is a second cast of it in the
gardens by the Louvre in Paris). It is closely
related to Maillol's monument to Cézanne
of 1921–5, a fact which points, not to any
weakening of his creative powers, but
rather to a need for 'archetypal' forms of
expression which yet (and this is highly
characteristic of Maillol) remain warm-

blooded, concrete and human.

Maillol began as a painter and in 1893 he
founded a tapestry workshop. Not until
1901 did he devote himself entirely to
sculpture, being compelled by an eye-
complaint to make this choice. His sculptural form was determined by modelling
and tactile feeling and although he made
some sculptures in wood and stone, he was
no pure carver, but a modeller through and
through. His sculptures are completely at
home in the bright but never burning light
of the Mediterranean (he lived at Banyuls
sur Mer).

AUGUSTE RODIN
(1840–1917, France)

Squatting woman
bronze, 95 × 73 × 60 cm, 1882

This *Squatting woman* is one of the figures
Rodin used, in a somewhat different form,
in his *Gate of hell* (c.1880–1917): it can, in fact,
be said that a great many of the sculptures
he made during those last thirty years were
related to the *Gate* which, as a result of endless financial and technical complications,
took so much more time than those who
had commissioned it (the Ministère des
Beaux-Arts) had ever envisaged.

The *Squatting woman,* later also called *La
Luxure,* is bending over towards a man who
is falling backwards. The title *Gate of hell* is
taken from a canto in the *Inferno* of Dante's
Divina Commedia. Rodin saw hell as the
place of exile for all those who were driven
on by their erotic sins and desires: his hell is
not created by a deity, but by man himself.
This approach runs parallel to many of the
themes in Baudelaire's *Fleurs du Mal,* which
was published in 1857.

The passion driving the figures gave
Rodin the maximum possibility of
breaking through contours, of creating a
play of light and shade rich in strong contrasts and of taking extreme risks with
balance. At this period there came to the
fore many sculptural problems he had been
grappling with in the preceding years, such
as how far equilibrium can be disturbed,
muscles strained and emotional pathos
given expression without the sculptural
form being destroyed.

HENRY MOORE
(b.1898, England)

Three standing motifs, Nos. 1, 2, 7
bronze, h.320, 320 and 334 cm, 1955–56

Henry Moore's sculptural group was unveiled in April 1965 outside the actual museum terrain on the edge of the game preserve of the Hoge Veluwe National Park. The place had been chosen by Moore himself near to the foundations of what was once to have been the large museum designed by Henry van de Velde.

The *Three standing motifs* were selected by the sculptor from a long series of studies on which he had been working since 1955, when he had been asked to make a sculpture for the courtyard of a building in Milan. A solitary poplar tree near this building gave him the idea of trying to find a vertical form which would contrast with the pronounced horizontality of its architecture. It was not until later on that the idea of a crucifixion scene occurred to him and this is in fact an interpretation (or rather, an association) that came from the spectators more than from the artist himself. He still continued to work on the theme after 1956. It reached a point of rest in the *Three figures in front of a wall* of 1959.

The base – designed by the artist himself – bears a certain formal relationship to the museum foundations. Moore was deeply moved by Mrs. Kröller's dream of building a museum at precisely this spot, where the game preserve with its expanses of sand and scattered pine trees meet the park area, where massive beeches and oaks give the landscape a completely different character. Her intention of bringing art, nature and architecture into harmony in the National Park finds clear expression in this situation.

MARK DI SUVERO
(b.1933, Italy, U.S.A.)

K-piece
iron (painted red), 12 × 12 × 6.30 m, 1972

Di Suvero was born in China where his anti-Fascist Italian parents lived for a time. At the age of seven he went to the United States where he has spent a large part of his nomadic existence. In his work he became fascinated by the precarious balance of heavy wooden or iron beams held in equilibrium in a seemingly clumsy way. Like his parents he has been opposed from the very beginning to any form of constraint, the constraint of a fixed abode, of conventional methods of construction or a museum setting. By reason of their size, their weight and their daring construction, his works can only be placed out of doors and they can only be made in factories or shipyards and created in collaboration with the workers. Because of all this a peak period for him was that (1972–4) he spent in Chalon sur Saône, living in a boat near a shipyard where, with the workers there, he made a series of six large and several small sculptures. And it was also entirely characteristic of him that, afterwards, the piece of sculpture to remain in Chalon was chosen by the people of Chalon themselves.

After that began his triumphal progress through the official art world, with exhibitions in the Jardins des Tuileries in Paris and in the Whitney Museum and the streets of New York, plus an illustration on the cover of *Time*.

CHAIM JACOB LIPCHITZ
(1891–1973, Russia, France, U.S.A., Israel)

Le Chant des voyelles
bronze, h. 395 cm, 1931–32

With the theme of *Le Chant des voyelles* Lipchitz was reaching out for a motif (the relationship between man and musical instrument) that was repeatedly used by the Cubists. However, while the Cubists often incorporated stringed instruments into their works in such a way that the body of the instrument almost seems to have become fused with that of the player, with Lipchitz the relationship is more complex and intense. He, too, portrays a symbiosis between stringed instrument (harp) and human body, but with him the couple become a harp and their union music, primeval song. His sculptures of this period show a perfect balance between mass and opening, their structure being built up in a parallel arrangement. The explosive power often shown by his later work is here kept completely under control.

Lipchitz more than once used subjects taken from the Old Testament or Greek mythology as a means of expression *(e.g. Jacob and the Angel, David and Goliath, Prometheus and the Vulture, The rape of Europa)*. This identification with images from literature enabled him on the one hand to give expression to his great perturbation over the events going on around him (especially between 1932 and 1945), while on the other he succeeded in establishing a creative distance by removing the conflict to a 'timeless period'. However, during those years he time and again depicted violent conflict or physically violent wrestling.

CHAIM JACOB LIPCHITZ
(1891–1973, Russia, France, U.S.A., Israel)

The couple
bronze, 92 × 163 × 96 cm, 1928–29

In the period when he was working on *The couple* (in various formats and different versions), Lipchitz developed away from Cubist form, but his need for a summarization in a single large – abstracted – form was still strong. In this sculpture he anticipated his works of the thirties, which portray the coming together of two figures, either in harmony *(the Return of the Prodigal Son)* or in destruction *(Prometheus strangling the vulture).*

From a series of *Transparencies* he made between 1928 and 1930 it became clear to him how important the relationship is between mass and opening, light and shadow, and in the twofold unity of the two figures, who in their coupling either lose their individuality or experience it in a heightened form, he was able to express this formal relationship in a very direct way. There is no asymmetry here and no dominance or subjugation of any one sculptural element, but a form which is full of movement and nowhere rigid or schematic and through which the configuration composed of two elements becomes a

single monumental sign reduced to its essentials. The extremely powerful curve of the legs, which is continued in arms and head, is kept within bounds by the long line of the back, while at the head end the heavy mass of the arms conducts all the power inwards and keeps it under control. This power contained within the contours is characteristic of all Lipchitz' work up to 1940. Thereafter, following his flight to America, a new element makes an appearance – the curve begins to gain the upper hand.

DAME BARBARA HEPWORTH
(1903–75, England)

Quadrilaterals with two circles
bronze, h. 315 cm, 1964

On several occasions after 1960 Barbara
Hepworth made very large sculptures (*e.g.
Single form* of 1962–3 for the UNO building
in New York, a commission in memory of
Dag Hammerskjöld). They are characterized by the fact than in spite of their size
they still bear a considered relationship to
the human figure or, to put it better, the
human field of vision. The theme of quadrilaterals with circles evokes reminiscences
of the period of the journal *Unit one* (1931)

and the collection of essays *Circle* (1937),
when, mainly as a result of the inspiration
of Naum Gabo who was living in London
at the time, a group of artists living in
England were working on the basis of a
Constructivist concept, *i.e.* concentrating
on essentially geometrical, abstract form.
(On the Continent, too, various groups
were formed at that time of artists working
in the same way, who often had close contacts with architects and natural philoso-
phers.)

This revival of a Constructivist theme:
the relationship between rectangle (or
square) and circle, also cropped up in 1966,
when Hepworth made a series of little

maquettes in marble and schist of small
rectangular forms with round openings,
whereby she placed the forms one behind
the other (in echelon) or piled them up by
twos. The large marble version that came
into being out of these 'formal exercises' is
in the Boymans-van Beuningen Museum
in Rotterdam. In that year, 1966, (as in
1933–36), Hepworth was continuously
occupied with the relationships of forms to
each other and that of closed form to pierced form. However, the rectangle or square
is exceptional in the development of her
work, since she virtually always worked in
flowing curves and rounded forms.

RICHARD SERRA
(b.1939, U.S.A.)

Spin Out for Robert Smithson
3 plates in Cor-tèn steel, 250 × 1200 × 4 cm,
1973

While Serra was engaged on this work in the sculpture park, he heard that his friend Robert Smithson had crashed in his helicopter while inspecting a Land Art project in Nevada, so he dedicated the *Spin Out* to Smithson as a memorial. Serra came to Otterlo several times to select a place in the sculpture garden. After taking careful measurements of the dell and undertaking months of research at home, he decided on this installation: the three heavy steel 'walls' inserted into the mounds create the possibility of a completely different spatial experience. The serene dell with the low ridge on one side and the high, heavily wooded mounds on the other assumes a totally different character with the coming into being of a rotating movement from narrowing to widening.

The peace of the dell is disturbed, but not destroyed, while the weathering process undergone by the steel is important too. Over the years the outer skin flakes off and thus the colour also changes, so that there arises a parallel between the variations in nature in the different seasons and the weathering of the steel.

Serra has been active in various artistic fields (*arte povera,* film, television), but his interest has always centred on processes, while of recent years intervention in a landscape has in particular become of great importance to him. This always involves activating, not destroying a given situation.

DAME BARBARA HEPWORTH
(1903–75, England)

Sphere with internal form
bronze, h. 101.5 cm, 1963

In 1931, the year in which she created her first pierced forms, Barbara Hepworth was already searching for an abstraction of the human figure. The *Sphere with internal form* of thirty years later incorporates two themes that are of great importance throughout her whole oeuvre: the small form resting inside a large, enclosing form and the piercing. The piercing of a form has various functions. It is not only a penetration into the core of the mass, whereby light is admitted into it and clearly serves a purpose by contrast to the darkness of the mass. The light plays on the inner surface and – if the sculpture is of wood or stone – follows the course of veins and sinews. The respect Barbara Hepworth had for materials, which she never forced or approached in an ambiguous way, was always coupled with a desire for knowledge, with reflection on the organic laws and natural growth of those materials. Thus the piercing of them was both a sculptural and a mental activity. The relationship of the sculpture to the forces of nature that act upon it (wind, water, light) plays a major role too: the light does not only play over and burnish the outer surface, but it also as it were forms the sculpture from the inside outwards. This feeling for the effect of light was, of course, innate, but Barbara Hepworth's perception of the effect of light was further strengthened at such moments in her life as her stay in Italy on a study grant (in 1924–25), a lengthy visit to Provence with Ben Nicholson (1932) and intensely experienced visits to Venice (1950) and Greece (1954).

LUCIO FONTANA
(1899–1968, Argentina, Italy)

Concetto spaziale nature (5 spheres)
bronze, diam. 97, 92, 92, 102, 110 cm,
1959–60

Fontana was one of the first artists after the Second World War (as early as 1948) to formulate in words and images how unstable the balance is between solid material and forces in space. This drama is played out in his paintings, in which the canvas is perforated by cuts or holes caused by his gestures. Only once did he express the idea in bronze: five large spheres eaten away by destructive forces from within or without – it is impossible to tell which. As in volcanic craters and fissures the mass has opened up and the curling edges evince the searing forces that are attacking them. Both the size of the spheres and the violence of the splits lend these forms a daemonic power which is weakened or perhaps perverted in the paintings by the aesthetic value of the colours of the oil paint.

Fontana was far in advance of other artists in his work. He was already experimenting with light-areas in 1949 and he worked with an architect on environments. In the war years he remained in his native Argentina where he provided his young compatriots with great inspiration and *élan*.

PHILLIP KING
(b.1934, Tunis, England)

Reel I

steel and aluminium, painted red and green,
167.6 × 381 × 426.7 cm, 1968

This is probably one of the sculptures in which King comes closest to the artist he admires, Matisse. It does this not only by reason of the radiant, weightless colours, red and green, or the long melodic curves that are broken by straight lines in only a few places, but also because of the open inner space which is so characteristic of

King's work and plays an important part in that of Matisse as well (see, for example, the *Serpentinatas* in bronze and the painting *The dance*). King's work has a strong relationship to man (scale, positioning, surveyability) and to nature: 'sculpture is about breathing in and breathing out'. The way in which contact with the earth is achieved, the tension between the force of gravity and the desire to float and between opaque and transparent materials in his assemblages of bricks, steel girders and grids, all indicate that he is not concerned with 'alienation' and the artificial, but rather with the trans-

formation of the given facts of nature, a parallel with nature. In this colour is very important: colour that has reflective power and is not absorbed by the material, but lives in the space between the spectator and the sculpture. Like so many other English sculptors, King worked and taught for a period in the sixties at the St. Martin's School of Art in London. However, the effect he had there was less far-reaching and more remote than that of Anthony Caro, who radically influenced the development of English sculpture.

ANDRÉ VOLTEN
(b.1925, Netherlands)

Pillar
stainless steel, h.850 cm, diam. 65 cm, 1968

Volten mostly works in series, that is to say, certain sculptural or, better still, constructional problems are posited as themes and carried through so far that a saturation point is reached. In 1967–68 he made a series of pillars in stainless steel in which the whole pillar, or part of it, is composed of a pile of rings with slight shifts in their positioning. Because of the high polish and strong light-catching property of the material these shifts create a vibrating break in the lines of light and shadow.

The building up of similar or identical elements is a factor that has recurred time and time again in Volten's work since 1960, with the result that his entire oeuvre exhibits an impressive coherence. He very often takes a cube or a cylinder (tubes) as his starting-point, but on occasion he may also use a sphere. His great technical perfection and the effect produced by each small intervention on the hard material (stainless steel, brass or polished granite) give his work a power which, through his immense concentration, also demands of the spectator an understanding of the logic, the perfectionism and the authenticity of his way of working. These qualities make his works eminently suitable for placing beside buildings, albeit they often act as an inexorable touchstone for the quality of the architecture around them. Volten is firmly convinced that artists can and must play a part in any discussion or planning undertaken by town-planners and landscape architects.

CAREL N. VISSER
(b.1928, Netherlands)

Double form
iron, 160 × 300 cm, 1958

The double forms that Visser made in 1957–58 are in fact descendants of the theme of 'mating birds' of 1953–54. This development was not, however, a process that took place step by step, but after the first small naturalistic sculpture of 1953, which was a direct recollection of storks mating on the roof of his childhood home, Visser made a variant the following year in which he already achieved a radical abstraction. The bird forms were stiffened and formalized and became mirror-images of each other, while the space between them became very important. In the years that followed this process of abstraction continued, in various formats and (which is typical of Visser) build-ups (horizontal or vertical).

It is clear that other remembered images, other associations, then began to influence the bird theme and as a result the compositions became more complex, but without losing the basic image and mirror-image idea. Visser's work shows a good many intermediate stages, a good many versions of a single theme, and it is thus very illuminating in respect of making the spectator aware of the richness of the creative process (the work of the English sculptor Armitage is also a good example of such a gradual, complex growth).

The titles of the sculptures sometimes refer to the concrete remembered image and sometimes to the sculptural activity, the geometrical abstraction. As his material Visser invariably chooses iron with its granular surface that reacts to the weather and is always changing.

CAREL N. VISSER
(b.1928, Netherlands)

Cube and its piling up
iron, 200 × 200 cm, 200 × 225 cm, 1967

A second formal theme that predominates in Visser's work is that of the cube: a hard solid cube that is 'sawn' and shifted into layers, a cube of limp plates of iron that lean against one another or even a cube that has fallen apart and is lying on the ground.

In the early years of this development (1966 and 1967) the (small) cubes were piled up or placed in series one after the other. They were also welded together, hanging on a horizontal iron beam. In his woodcuts and drawings, which are not studies for his sculptures, but which always accompany his three-dimensional work, Visser made very beautiful compositions of open, linked cubes.

In 1969 he began working with limp plates of iron joined together by pieces of leather and in 1976 with limp bands of iron and finally with strips of leather that he lets fall on the ground in a completely arbitrary way to form chance configurations. What the next development will be we do not know as yet, but it is almost unthinkable that he will completely abandon the iron that responds so well to his vision. What is a possibility is that this turning to very flexible material will result in an enrichment of his formal themes. But, as he himself says of his sculptures: 'They are in my head and the only way I can get them out of it is to make them sometime'.

TONY SMITH
(1912–80, U.S.A.)

Wandering rocks: dud, slide, crocus, shaft, smohawk

steel, c.57 × 21.5 × 79 cm, c.57 × 193 × 70 cm, c.120 × 114 × 69 cm, c.183 × 114 × 70 cm, c.70 × 120 × 57 cm, 1967

Each of the five elements of *Wandering rocks* is based on the same module and together they would form a compact block. Smith got the idea for this work from looking at blocks of stone in a Japanese garden. At the time he was intensively preoccupied with the relationship between his sculptures and their surroundings, whether indoors or out, seeking for flexibility in the arrangement of work that consisted of a number of different elements and for the possibility of the spectator's gaining a varying experience of the forms and their relationships by walking through the sculpture. In other words his way of looking was that of an architect, which is, in fact, what he was from 1937 to 1960.

He gave his *Wandering rocks* to the Kröller-Müller Museum because he found it an ideal setting for his work, a point which is mentioned here because there are numerous sculptors (Arp, Lipchitz, Hepworth, Paolozzi, Di Suvero, Serra, Dubuffet, Ad Dekkers, etc.) who have given work to the museum or waived a fee for the reason that their work comes into its own so perfectly in the sculpture park or the museum building itself. For this we have to thank the architecture of Van de Velde and Quist, which is so entirely at the service of the collection, and the lay-out of the sculpture park, which was conceived of by Professor Bijhouwer as a series of open grassy areas (= rooms) surrounded by trees and bushes.

EVERT STROBOS
(b.1943, Netherlands)

Palissade
Cor-tèn steel, h.8 m, 24 elements, 1973

Strobos spent two years (1972–73) working with the same long elements: first in four different places indoors in stainless steel and then in the sculpture park at Otterlo in Cor-tèn steel. In Amsterdam he made a construction in tent form with the sharp ends of the elements resting on the floor. In Groningen, Dordrecht and Enschede the constructions were less open, the elements being focussed on a wall and the ceiling. In Otterlo the 'palissade' finally acquired a permanent arrangement with the elements placed in a curved line with their sharp ends on the grass, while the broad ends were welded together at the top. Since the screen composed of the elements faces east, long lines of light and shadow are formed on the grass around it and the sculpture thus acquires a duplication which changes with the position of the sun.

After 1973 Strobos introduced a new element into his work: he still started with the same long metal elements, but he snapped them at certain levels like reeds that have bent over without completely breaking off. He is inspired by architecture and nature to the same degree and he always seeks for contact with both without excluding either.

CLAES OLDENBURG
(b.1929, Sweden, U.S.A.)

Trowel
steel sprayed blue, 1170 × 365 cm, 1971–76

Oldenburg made the *Trowel* originally (in 1971) for an exhibition in Sonsbeek Park, Arnhem. It was afterwards bought for the museum, where, during restoration in 1976 the form was altered somewhat and the original aluminium paint was replaced by a bright blue coating.

Oldenburg had already been turning over the idea of making a trowel since 1969, but it was in Sonsbeek Park itself that, as he looked at the (mole?) hills, the plan took on definitive form. His sculptures are always based on the observation of perfectly ordinary objects: a lipstick, an ice bag, a clothes peg, etc. By monumental enlargement or by making them in flexible materials he creates an alienating effect: the *Trowel* keeps the form of a rowel in the main and its position suggests the normal function of a trowel, but to it there has been added – literally – an artificial facet (material, colour, size) and it is that which determines the total impression.

Going to America as a child (his father was Ambassador), the sight of all these typically American objects, whose names he did not know and which he had never seen in use, must have made an indelible impression on him. In his 'Maus-Museum' he has assembled a collection of all the things, in their normal manifestations that held him spellbound to such an extent that he needed to 'enlarge them out' in this monumental way, in order to rid himself of the memory of them.

KENNETH SNELSON
(b.1927, U.S.A.)

Needle tower
aluminium, stainless steel
28 × 5.40 m, 1968

Under the inspiration of the work and
lectures of Buckminster Fuller, Snelson
arrived (in 1948) step by step at the development of his tensegrity-system: a configuration of aluminium tubes held in suspension
by a taut steel cable and with a minimal
supporting point (three feet in this case) on
the ground. The name 'tensegrity' was
coined by Fuller, but it was Snelson who
gradually envolved the system out of
playful mobile constructions.

The *Needle tower* is the tallest construction by him in a public collection and precisely because it is placed among more
'conventional' sculptures, it makes the
public appreciate how difficult it is to
define the boundaries of the fine arts. Time
and time again the *métier* of the artist over-
laps those of the engineer, the constructor
and the mathematician, to take only
Snelson's field. Beauty is not the sole prero-
gative of the work of art, but what is an
essential factor is the difference in function.
The tower is the crystallization of a
rationally built up train of thought, but it is
its complete lack of purpose by comparison
with what we like to term functional construction, which can be just as elegant and
beautiful (bridges, columns, models of
crystals, etc.), that makes it a work of art.
Snelson took out a patent on his tensegrity-
system and the fact that it was granted him
shows how much the interwovenness of
constructional and artistic processes is
recognized at present as entirely real.

CORNELIUS ROGGE
(b.1932, Netherlands)

Tent project
canvas, metal, rope, h.170–650 cm,
diam. 210–675 cm, 1975

With the installation of these six tents in the sculpture park Rogge got the chance for the first time to realize an idea he had long been working on to scale. The name tent perhaps arouses wrong expectations: they are completely closed sculptural forms in canvas without a single entrance. Yet it is precisely this ambiguity that is inherent in the sculpture: it resembles a tent, but it is not one. A tent affords protection to whoever enters it, but here the protection is given to an inner space that cannot be entered or come into contact with, but can only be experienced in the imagination. In the course of time the material disintegrates and perhaps wears away and sand drifts on to the terraces where grass – with great difficulty – begins to grow. Nor is it only the material that is attacked by the forces of nature, but the form of the sculpture can only hold its own – in the material sense – with great difficulty and not in any lasting way. This conflict, or better, this situation is the basis of Rogge's entire oeuvre. He does not feel it to be tragic. On the contrary, he sees it as the essence of his artistry to portray the conflict, and then not only the transitoriness, but also the need on the one hand to put up a fight against the depredations and on the other to accept the limits of this defence. It is, in addition, characteristic of Rogge that he expresses the conflict between realization and transitoriness not only in images, but also in words.

DAVID VAN DE KOP
(b.1937, Netherlands)

Tûam
steel plates, sand, grass, height 250 cm ×
length plates 850 cm × total length 600 cm,
1974

The *Tûam* (Celtic for barrow) was made on a site determined and chosen by Van de Kop himself. Like a dyke it cuts through a long and narrow stretch of grass in the sculpture park, which is bounded on one side by a tall rhododendron wood and on the other by the solid ridge with beech trees that forms the natural boundary of the sculpture park. Van de Kop is fascinated by the fight the forces of nature (the growing-power of the grass on the tumulus) put up against the weight, the counter-pressure of heavy metal plates positioned by man. The sand is pressed away by the heavy steel, but in its turn the weight of the sand exerts counter-pressure: the steel plates are not closed up together, but give way at the top and a path comes into being over the tumulus. This typically Dutch trial of strength between man and nature is the basic theme of Van de Kop's work. Although he is related in this to the artists in America and England who make their mark on the landscape (Heizer, Serra, Richard Long, etc.), his work is much more concentrated on the effects of pressure and counter-pressure, of compressing and coercing within bounds. As studies for his projects he makes splendid collages of photographs and drawings or paper forms and drawings.

FRITZ WOTRUBA
(1907–1975, Austria)

Relief
marble, 210 × 75 cm, 1960

With the utmost singlemindedness Wotruba sought throughout his life for a sculptural form which seems to stem from early Cubism, but which in reality – with the aid of the material – completely met his personal need to concentrate on elementary forms and relationships. Although he also made many sculptures in bronze, he was pre-eminently a stone-carver and he confined himself to four themes: standing, sitting, reclining and walking, often expressed in a single figure, but sometimes (especially in the case of standing) in more than one.

The rigorous limitations he imposed in respect of his own work were coupled with a great openness to the work of others, in the fields of theatre, music and literature as well as plastic arts (he was a great friend of Alban Berg, Musil, Canetti and Hermann Broch). Within the framework he laid down for himself he achieved great monumentality and cogency. His work for the theatre and opera, including decors for *Oedipus Rex, Oedipus at Colonnus* and *Der Ring der Nibelungen,* showed how powerfully his work dominated the area around it, in spite of, or precisely because of, its great reticence and intensity. His whole oeuvre shows a consistency and a concentration on one sculptural form (which had already become clearly apparent in his work by 1947) which are unique in the history of sculpture of the last thirty years.

JEAN DUBUFFET
(b.1901, France)

Jardin d'émail
concrete, epoxy paint, polyurethane,
20 × 30 m, 1973–74

In the east corner of the sculpture park, shut in by tall trees on two sides, lies the *Jardin d'émail*: an area made of concrete, capricious in form and surrounded by high walls, which is painted with white paint and tortuous black lines, something absolutely unnatural in the middle of a park which is itself laid out in an informal way. In the concrete area there are also a 'tree' and two 'bushes' of polyurethane.

Throughout his life (including the periods when he was exclusively occupied with the wine trade) Dubuffet has concentrated on the essence and the boundaries of art (not only the fine arts, but music and poetry as well). In so doing he has consistently opted for chaos, for *art brut*: the art of children, psychotics and amateurs (although his own use of language is intensely erudite, poetic and lucid).

The *Jardin d'émail* is one of a small series of projects of recent years, in which Dubuffet has depicted the chaotic, disorientating and inexplicable in three-dimensional form. Entering through a narrow opening in the trunk of a tree, visitors are practically blinded by the shining whiteness and the black lines, which resemble outlines, but which run differently from what one would expect (*e.g.* just over the treads of the steps). Dubuffet's hope is that people will manage to remain quietly in the *Jardin d'émail* until the penetrating power (the vital necessity) of this chaotic or, better, unformed aspect of creativity can come through to them.